Replace Your *Grand Illusions* with **Grander Realities**

Replace Your *Grand Illusions* with *Grander Realities*

BILLY RIGGS

**Executive
Books**

Replace Your Grand Illusions With Grander Realities

Published by
Executive Books
206 West Allen Street
Mechanicsburg, PA 17055

Cover design by Don Day

ISBN: 0-937539-72-4

Printed in the United States of America

Dedicated to my wife,

Trish,

whose love is a reality
grander than any illusion.

Acknowledgments

Special thanks to my agent, **Jim Chism,** and his wife Janet, who risked and sacrificed so much to promote and market an unknown and untested motivational speaker and illusionist named Billy Riggs in 1996. Thanks also to their colleagues at Awesome Speakers Bureau in San Antonio, Texas: Dave Galbraith, Kae Diotte, Kristeen Sooy, and Rick Boynton. Your investment in my life is deeply appreciated and never forgotten.

Contents

Contents

Chapter 1

Grand Illusions

April 20, 1999 dawned as many other spring days in Littleton, Colorado. That sunny Tuesday morning was greeted by sixty-degree temperatures and visions of summer break only three weeks away. Hundreds of students and faculty members of Columbine High School dressed, ate breakfast, and departed for classes under a grand, if mundane, illusion that today would be just another school day. But by noon they—and an entire nation—would be deeply *dis*illusioned. Students Eric Harris and Dylan Klebold shattered the veneer of tranquility that day with a hail of gunfire that left fourteen students and one faculty member dead, hundreds deeply shaken, and millions awakened—all too late—to something I call "grand reality."

The haunting fact is that the Columbine High School disaster could have been avoided. Police had been warned months earlier that Eric Harris had published a web site threatening to slaughter his fellow students. The boy's parents had discovered detailed instructions for building a bomb in their garage. The two young assailants-to-be had produced a videotape for a class project depicting themselves wearing black trench coats while annihilating fellow students with machine guns *and showed it in class!* They had spoken openly of guns and revenge and Adolph Hitler, reveling in the supposed glory of their self-assigned appellation "The Trench Coat Mafia." Yet everyone—parents, teachers, police, and classmates alike—clung stubbornly to their illusion of security, preferring it to a less-than-pleasant reality. This propensity to choose comforting illusions over a potentially disquieting reality is mirrored in the daily lives of most people, though with much more subtle, yet no less horrifying, results.

Years ago my wife and I vacationed in the San Francisco area and browsed through some of the shops at the Embarcadero. There we witnessed a fascinating demonstration of a virtual reality game. A very large man stood in a round booth about the size of a kitchen table, with wires attached to various parts of his body. He carried a toy gun in each hand, and wore a virtual reality visor that covered most of his face. The gathered crowd watched with amusement as this man flailed madly about shooting at enemies no one else could see. For the sake of illustration, imagine for a moment that one of this man's mortal enemies was in the crowd with a baseball bat in hand. Further, pretend that this nemesis was a tiny man who could never survive a fist-fight with the hulk of a man wearing the visor. Nonetheless, in the described scenario the little underdog would easily be able to defeat his larger, stronger enemy, because in a battle the advantage always falls to those playing in the real world over those living in a fantasy. I saw in the man with the visor a parable of the human predicament, frantically shooting at imaginary enemies while leaving himself utterly vulnerable to real ones.

All of us travel through life wearing, as it were, a

virtual reality visor that impairs our perspective, distorts reality, and superimposes an imaginary world over the real one. Thus, the world we perceive is often quite different from the one that actually exists, presenting us with two alternatives from which to choose. We can cling stubbornly to our illusions, and thereby choose their devastating consequences when they turn to dust and pour through our fingers, as they inevitably will. Or we can take the road less traveled, choose to strip ourselves of those illusions, and reap the magnificent advantages of living life in the real world, seeing reality just as it is instead of viewing it through a set of distorting lenses I have come to call "Grand Illusions." Disillusionment, as it is used in this book, refers to the brave act of removing the virtual reality visor and choosing a sometimes unpleasant reality over a (temporarily) more comfortable illusion. Freedom, balance, and a decided advantage in the game of life are restored with the removal of these illusions.

This book is based on two fundamental assumptions. First, reality—even if painful—is better than our illusions. And secondly, reality will inevitably come sooner or later, as it did to those at Columbine High School. It will either be recognized and embraced voluntarily, in time to adjust to it, prepare for it, or even prevent it, or it will come crashing in upon us abruptly, involuntarily, unexpectedly, having already done irreparable damage. One of the keys to a happy and successful life is choosing to identify and eliminate one's illusions before their consequences have the opportunity to materialize as a painful and inescapable new reality.

Years ago I had a conversation with a close friend who had just discovered that her husband of three years had been cheating on her nearly all that time. She had separated from him and was preparing for divorce proceedings. "I'm so disillusioned right now," she sadly intoned.

"That's good," I replied, fully expecting the puzzled look with which she responded.

"What do you mean?" she asked. I explained how disillusionment, while rarely painless, is still much to be preferred to the only alternative: living another three, ten, or even thirty years under the illusion that she was investing her one-and-only life with the right man. I then asked what I believe to be a key question: "Don't you wish you had become disillusioned with this man six months before the wedding?"

"Absolutely," she replied. I conclude from her answer not just that disillusionment is much to be preferred to an illusion, but that *the sooner it comes to any of us, the better off we are.*

It is not that our illusions, by themselves, are necessarily harmful. It is the way they affect our behavior that renders them damaging, neutral, or potentially even helpful.[1] The impact of our mental myths is directly proportional to the stubbornness with which we cling to them, and the role they play in our decision-making processes. Which of us has not used the power of imagination as a catapult to pretended wealth, stardom, or irresistible sex appeal? But such daydreams that melt away with nothing more than the ringing of a nearby phone or the barking of a neighbor's dog are harmless. Those that resist years of therapy, though, are potentially ruinous. Most of our illusions lurk somewhere in the gray twilight between those two extremes, inflicting unnecessary pain and inducing otherwise avoidable trauma.

1 The rare, but considerable, potential benefits of illusions will be discussed in Chapter XI.

Choosing to live with one's illusions is generally unproductive, and at worst devastating. This is because an illusion, by definition, is a deception, an untruth. Therefore, to believe in one is foolish. For many years, as a professional magician, I have been creating classic illusions on stage, cutting women in pieces, floating them in the air, performing feats of apparent mind reading, etc. The audience *knows* that the woman has not actually been dismembered. But they are entertained by the fact that it *looks* like she has, and they have no idea how the illusion is created. Such illusions are *good*, for one simple reason: the audience recognizes them as exactly what they are, falsehoods. There is, therefore, no chance whatsoever that they will make any decisions based on the assumption that a woman really can be cut in half and put back together safely (thank heaven!). A harmless illusion is one that is acknowledged as such, and therefore will never affect anyone's decision-making processes.

However, on occasion I have been approached after a performance by a reality-challenged audience member who really believes that I utilize paranormal or spiritual forces on stage. I worry about these people. Because if they believe *I* use such powers (despite my open and unambiguous statements to the contrary), they are easy targets to be fleeced by con artists such as phone psychics, palm readers, mediums and their ilk. It is their penchant for illusions and their resistance to the truth that renders them vulnerable.

These people provide an excellent, even if extreme, example of how illusions can become the downfall of much saner and balanced people like those who might read this book. But *our* illusions, being far more subtle and difficult to detect, are potentially even more ruinous. Their power is in their reclusive nature. Concealed in the crevices of one's cerebellum from childhood they form a paradigm, a grid, a set of lenses through which we view our world and upon which we base life's most important and minuscule choices. And it is on such choices that life turns. Given life's myriad of choices, a person who lives under significant illusions is slowly, almost imperceptibly, taking his or her life in a direction that is quite probably catastrophic. Hence, one's most intractable illusions also constitute one's *destiny*.

Misconceptions and their harmful consequences form the core of almost every children's story, and every adult's life. Think of Hans Christian Andersen's king who believed he was wearing beautiful new clothes visible only to the wise, while he was actually unclothed. Remember Little Red Riding Hood who was almost done in when she fell for the wolf-dressed-as-grandmother routine. Consider Icarus who believed he could fly to the sun, only to fall to earth when his wax wings melted, or Chicken Licken who interpreted the drop of an acorn as the sky falling. For the lucky ones, surrendering to an illusion is merely embarrassing. For most it is debilitating or worse. These fairy tales all teach the same difficult lesson which will be reiterated again and again in this book: illusions are almost always dangerous and are to be eschewed as such. Perhaps more convincing are the fairy tales' parallels in the following true-to-life examples.

Members of "The People's Temple" lived under the illusion that psychopath Jim Jones was a prophet of God. Consequently, they followed him to their gruesome deaths in a hellhole in Guyana. Similarly, members of the "Heaven's Gate" sect genuinely believed a myth too absurd even for a fairy tale, that the Hale-Bopp comet cloaked a spaceship ready to beam them aboard as they took their own lives. Neville Chamberlain, former Prime Minister of Great

6

Britain, clung tenaciously to a fantasy that evil dictators could be trusted. Touting the illusion of "peace in our time," he credulously fell for Adolph Hitler's promise to cease further aggression in Europe, allowing the German Führer time to gain sufficient momentum to become nearly invincible, and to plunge the world into global conflict. Just as believing these chimeras resulted in tragic and unnecessary deaths, accepting your own mental myths as true will precipitate the death of your most precious dreams and treasured relationships.

Millions of people live and die under the illusion that they are helpless to control their own behavior, or that they are unlovable, or destined for mediocrity or even failure. Others agonize under the persistent imagination that they are physically unattractive, or socially unacceptable. Still others carry with them throughout life an abiding fear of being abandoned by those closest to them.

I once interviewed someone to work for me who was intelligent, highly motivated, and capable. For the purposes of this book, we will call her Susan. The only red flag on her resume was that she had moved to a new job every couple of years throughout her career. Nevertheless, she seemed to have a good explanation for each move, so I hired her anyway. True to form, she succeeded admirably, then marched into my office eighteen months later to explain that she had decided to resign. "Why?" I asked incredulously.

What reason did she give? *"No one appreciates me!"*

I was shocked. This, I knew, was untrue. We had expressed tremendous appreciation for her not only verbally, but also in action and in salary. How, then, could she be so mistaken? The answer, I realized, was what I have come to call her "Grand Illusion." As the result of a challenging upbringing with unloving parents she carried deep in her subconscious mind a single overarching illusion that she would never be genuinely loved and accepted. Consequently, she had mentally constructed an elaborate grid of filters designed to reinforce that illusion, and no amount of appreciation could ever convince her otherwise. Quite the contrary, all attempts to demonstrate appreciation to Susan were followed by curious behaviors on her part intended to *make* us reject her. The only solution to her vexing problem was *dis*illusionment, the voluntary acknowledgement and repudiation of the illusion, and the slow and taxing trip back into objective reality. Fortunately, my friend was willing to begin that arduous journey and eventually stayed with that organization as long as I did.

Disillusionment is always better than living under illusions. And it is a considerable cause for celebration when a wise person takes the time and effort to *voluntarily and proactively* identify his or her own illusions, and become disillusioned before circumstances suddenly and brutally do it for them. Failure to renounce one's illusions sets in motion a process with inevitably harmful consequences.

Chapter 2

Pay More Attention
to that Man Behind the Curtain!

The classic fantasy movie, *The Wizard of Oz,* provides an interesting parallel to the progression through which our illusions eventually become reality. The well-known key characters in the movie are the Scarecrow, the Tin Man, the Cowardly Lion, the Wizard of Oz and Dorothy, who were respectively brainless, heartless, gutless, faceless, and homeless.

This sequence reflects our universally human proclivity for thoughts (in the brain) to create feelings (in the "heart"), which in turn produce fears (in the gut), inducing the impulse to wear a mask over one's true face. The inevitable result is to find oneself without a home, lacking a safe harbor in which to be truly authentic.

Stated another way, what one genuinely believes in the mind—whether it is true or not—has a profound effect on the heart, that is, the emotions. In turn, these powerful feelings sometimes produce irrational fears, driving otherwise secure people to cower before their imagined threats. These mythological dangers then become the justification for role-playing, hiding behind a curtain while pretending to be powerful, important, significant, wealthy, loveable, or some other supposed enhancement of an all-too-mundane reality. The end of this deadly downward spiral is to be homeless, the proverbial "man without a country," one who is without a safe place to be exactly who he or she is rather than a caricature.

If I Only Had a Brain

All of us enter life as the intellectual equivalent of the Scarecrow in The Land of Oz. This is not to say that we are brainless, but that we are to a degree blank slates on which our parents, circumstances, and the environment will eventually write. While this *tabula rasa* (literally, "blank slate") school of thought advanced by philosopher John Locke has fallen into disrepute with the advent and advances of modern neuroscience, and while I certainly do not advocate the theory, the fact still remains that environment plays a major role in a person's development. Abusive parents, domestic turmoil, an encouraging teacher, a cataclysmic historical event, even a casual remark by an unknown person can write nearly indelible messages on the psyche. Such messages grow in our early years to later form "Grand Illusions," producing overriding emotions that are then dragged into and through adult life. These illusions give some people an inordinate level of sensitivity to the people and circumstances that surround them.

I have been convinced for many years that most people emerge from childhood with at least one "Grand Illusion," a distorted view of themselves and their place in the world through which all information is filtered. To be sure, reality is skewed to one degree or another for all of us. But due to each person's upbringing and circumstances, *it is uniquely skewed for each individual.* For some like my friend and co-worker, Susan, in the preceding chapter, circumstances have programmed them to view themselves as being unwanted. For others it is an overriding belief that they are destined for greatness. Still others have concluded that they are inadequate, or socially unacceptable. Some feel invisible, or worry that no one can be trusted. I have identified in this book six separate and distinct ways in which the human mind commonly twists reality.

A good illustration is an amusement park funhouse with half-a-dozen different specialty mirrors, one to make you look thin, another fat, another tall, another short, and so on. While there are (apparently) only six fundamental ways in which the mind distorts self-perception, there are a huge number of degrees to which the distortion can take place, and an incalculable number of combinations of the six.

If I Only Had a Heart

Problems of the mind almost always give birth to difficulties of the heart. In other words, what we think inevitably affects how we feel about ourselves, about others, and about life; mental scarecrows invariably become emotional tin men. Said another way, Grand Illusions produce dominant emotions, which create a hypersensitivity that is as predictable as it is mysterious.

It is helpful to think of most people as "emotionally sunburned." What is to most people a gentle tap on the shoulder is experienced as excruciating pain to one who has recently spent too much time in the sun. Likewise, warm water is perceived as scalding, and the usually pleasant prospect of a therapeutic massage becomes terrifying. It is my belief that nearly everyone is *emotionally* sunburned,

11

but only in an *isolated area* or two of the psyche, and these areas vary widely from person to person in accordance with formative experiences had in the early years of life. The dominant grand illusion determines the area of "sunburn," and the more deeply imbedded the illusion, the more severe the resulting pain will be.

For example, a verbal jab intended as a simple tease is received well by most, but for one who already imagines himself to be socially unacceptable the response is more likely to be anger, hurt, or embarrassment. For a few with severely sunburned sensors, the reaction could be rage, anguish, or humiliation. Being left off the invitation list to a friend's dinner party will cause almost anyone to ask questions like, "I wonder if she's mad at me, or doesn't like me any more?" But saner thoughts prevail, and more realistic explanations emerge: "I'll bet I forgot to tell her my business trip was postponed. She thinks I'm out of town." And these conclusions are deemed acceptable. But for one who suffers under the dominant illusion of being unlovable, the questions lead only to more questions, then to premature and often irrational conclusions, brooding, and even depression. One who lost a parent early in life to death, divorce, or desertion may develop the grand illusion that no one can be counted on, and that all relationships are tenuous and conditional. Consequently, this person may interpret a spouse's late nights at the office as an affair, spelling the beginning of the end of a relationship that was, they imagine, destined for failure from the start.

If I Only Had the Nerve

The dominant emotion each person harbors, in turn, begets a predictable and almost inconsolable fear that lurks in the recesses of the mind throughout life for most people.

This "phantom fear," as I have come to refer to it, could perhaps be identified and measured with a polygraph. A subject could be fitted with strategically located electrodes, and a series of words could be read aloud. Words like unlovable, abandonment, unwelcome, failure, rejection, insignificance, unattractive, and invisible would be prominent on such a list. With most of the words, the needle would register little or no response. But with one or two (and *which* one or two varies with each person), the needle would swing noticeably. For some, it would "peg," that is, in meter-readers' parlance, deflect beyond the farthest possible degree of the meter to accurately measure it. The degree of deflection would, of course, correlate with how deeply imbedded the illusion and corresponding phantom fear have become.

I call it a "phantom fear" because it is almost entirely imaginary and unfounded, at least at the time it is formed. For instance, while all of us harbor strong distaste for rejection, we have also known individuals who suffer from an *inordinate* fear of it, one for which there is no readily apparent explanation. Likewise, there are those who are extremely self-conscious about their appearance, even though they may be quite good-looking to any objective observer. Delightful people live in silent agony that their friends or spouse will suddenly and inexplicably desert them. Their fears are quite common, perhaps even normal, but the degree to which they feel them is anything but normal. It is greatly heightened, and often for no discernible reason.

This factor is created by the different speeds with which our minds and emotions react to various stimuli, and later return to normal. To use a military example, our armed forces normally operate at "Defense Condition 5," known more briefly as "Defcon 5", which indicates a peacetime state of affairs. Progressively lower numbers indicate a greater degree of alertness, culminating with Defcon 1, maximum readiness for full-scale war. When an apparent threat suddenly intrudes into our lives, such as a mischievous friend jumping from behind a bush and shouting "Boo!," both our minds and emotions instantaneously jump from Defcon 5 to Defcon 1. We are instantly ready to fight or flee, whichever seems more appropriate to our central nervous system at that moment. A few tenths of a second later, once the "threat" has been recognized as a hoax, the mind returns to Defcon 5. *But the emotions linger at 1!* The heart continues to pound, adrenalin races through the blood stream, breathing remains shallow and rapid, muscles stay tense. And ever so slowly, the emotional scale retreats to Defcon 5, peace.

Many years ago I was driving down Interstate 95 in Georgia when suddenly a car ahead of me swerved, spun completely around, and came to a sliding halt in the grass median, upright and unscathed. I, along with several other travelers on the same highway, stopped to offer help. I was one of the first to reach the car, and asked the lady in the driver's seat if she was okay. She was visibly shaken, but bore no signs of injury. Still in a state of near panic, she blurted out, "I fell asleep!" Some thoughtful people who arrived at her car seconds after I did offered her a bottle of water. She politely refused, thanked them for their offer, and said, "I'm okay. I just need to sit here for a while and recover." *Recover?* Recover from what? She was not injured, and her car was unharmed, save a little less rubber on its tires. It was obvious what she meant. While she knew in her mind that she was now safe, her emotional state had not yet returned to normal. Her brain had, in a matter of seconds, gone from Defcon 5 to Defcon 1, then back again. But her emotions would take much longer to recover. This difference in the speed with which our minds and emotions recover is a critical factor in understanding why we behave the way we do.

Imagine for a moment you had scores of supposed "friends," whose sole mission in life was to hide behind doors, under beds and in closets with the intent of startling you. Several times each day, at the moments you least expect they would spring from their hiding places, shout "Boo!" and send your emotional meter off the scale. While your mind would quickly settle back to Defcon 5, recognizing that no danger exists and that these pranksters pose no physical threat at all, your emotions would never have the opportunity to return to normal before being ratcheted up once more. They would become forever "stuck" at 3 or 2, and with each successive fright the already over-stimulated emotions would "peg." In this way events that cause most people to move from 5 to 3 on their emotional meter, cause these "stuck" individuals to move from 3 to 1, or even beyond. The telltale sign is that their response is often completely inappropriate and disproportional to the actual circumstance.

If I Only Had a Life

Most people attempt to cope with their fears by avoiding them. They wisely avoid taking walks alone down deserted streets in the dangerous parts of town. They cautiously steer clear of rattlesnakes in the wild. They hold dutifully to handrails on steep stairwells. This, of course, is a normal and laudable means of handling *genuine* fears. But avoidance is a foolish way to handle *phantom* fears, ones that actually pose no threat at all. But the "emotionally sunburned" person is often unable to distinguish between a stroll with friends in Manhattan's Central Park on a sunny, crowded day and a walk alone through the deserted park late at night. Both hold equal terror for them. Avoiding the park altogether does, indeed, protect them from their fear of being mugged, but it also robs them of the benefits afforded by the park. A better strategy for handling phantom fears is clearly called for.

A common strategy for avoiding phantom fears rather than effectively eliminating them is *pretense*. For example, when the Wizard of Oz feared that his country charm was inadequate for ruling a city, he went to great lengths to create the illusion of power. Hiding behind a curtain, frantically pulling levers and turning cranks, he posed as one impervious to the charge of being inadequate or weak. The Brainless, Heartless, and Gutless have now predictably become *Faceless*. The mask chosen by any given individual will represent that person's attempt to avoid his or her phantom fear, a tendency that will be explored in detail in the next chapter. For now, suffice it to say that the price of wearing a mask is high. It is frequently paid in the currency of exhaustion, addiction and loneliness.

If I Only Had a Home

Perhaps an absurd illustration will be enlightening. Suppose that you were to feel an overwhelming desire to be perceived as a rabbit. Your first order of business would be to purchase a rabbit costume. But merely acquiring such a disguise would be the easy part; the costume must now and forever be regularly cleaned, pressed, and maintained. You would also have to change the way in which you travel, abjuring walking in favor of "hopping" around the office each day. You would have no choice but to alter your diet, trading in your filet mignon for carrots and lettuce. You would need, as well, to have a *huge* family! All of these steps would be essential to the task of maintaining the facade, and the strain of doing so would be tiring beyond words.

The longer the veneer is held in place, the wider the resultant gap between the public persona and the private self grows, ultimately becoming a yawning chasm which threatens to swallow the pretender. Eventually, those who wear masks and play roles long to be alone. They dread contact with others people because in the presence of others they must take great pains to preserve their "rabbit" image. Life has become a stage on which they perform a live juggling act, a frenzied performance from which the only respite is solitude. Anyone who might get too close must be pushed away, for fear that they'll notice the fake whiskers, or see a bit of human flesh along the edges of the eye holes, and ask, "Are you *really* a rabbit?" They have befallen the same fate as the Wizard of Oz, isolated, playing the part of his own driver and doorman, hiding behind a curtain designed to keep others at arm's length in order to avoid exposure. But there, behind that curtain, there is a visceral, if inauthentic, sense of solace and peace.

There, behind the curtain they can peel away the rabbit fur and feel the air on their skin. There, they can walk unencumbered, as a human being should. There, they can eat lasagna and enchiladas and apple pie *a la mode*. There, they can voice their real opinions, even if only to *themselves*. There, and only there, they can be themselves. Ironically, by acting like the Wizard, they have become like Dorothy, homeless. There is no community, no family, no safe and secure place where they can be accepted, embraced and loved for who they really are. Hiding behind his curtain, The Wizard has become the quintessential "man without a country".

It is there, behind the curtain, that life gradually begins to unravel. The exhaustion of wearing the mask, coupled with the lonesome existence it mandates, becomes the breeding ground for a host of destructive habits. Bereft of intimate relationships and the freedom that comes from authenticity, a vacuum is left in the "homeless" individual's personality. Into the vortex of this vacuum a thousand methods of self-destruction may be drawn. In desperate need of personal contact, but unable to take the "risk" of genuine intimacy, a secret life of affairs, hiring of prostitutes, or pornography addiction begins. In urgent need of pleasure to offset the drudgery of the never-ending vaudeville act that has become his public life, the modern-day Wizard of Oz retreats into compulsive gambling, shoplifting, or over-spending. The exigent desire for relief leads him into alcoholism, drug addiction, or a host of other escapes intended to temporarily deaden the pain. The eventual collapse of such a person is inevitable. Whether through medical problems, public humiliation, or arrest, exposure is unavoidable. It is inescapable because the relief that comes with exposure is the subconscious *goal* of the behavior that causes the disintegration of one's life.

Man's Best Friend

For me, the hero of *The Wizard of Oz* is the little dog, Toto. What the Wizard has feared most—exposure as a mere mortal—is revealed by the crafty canine to be more liberating than terrifying. His curtain turns out to be more of a self-imposed prison than a protective shield. By merely pulling back the curtain, Toto has set the Wizard free to enjoy the full benefits of relationships, authentic living, and *reality*. Within minutes of his exposure, his frightening persona has been transformed into one of generosity and encouragement. And he is soon on his way... *home*.

For this reason, I offer the following advice: "Pay *more* attention to that man behind the curtain." Pay enough attention, indeed, to recognize the curtain as the inevitable jail cell created by those who choose to live their lives as illusionists. And pay enough attention to perceive disillusionment as your last and best hope for a jailbreak, your final opportunity to disrupt the relentless inertia of your illusions as they strive to become a frightening and agonizing reality.

Chapter 3

The Inertia of an Illusion

In the early part of the nineteenth century, there was but one province of India not subject to British rule. The state of Kolhapur was instead governed by a rajah with more pressing problems than the threat of a British invasion, for his kingdom was routinely pillaged by a group of marauding bandits known only as "The Thugs." They came by night to steal from the treasury, murder citizens, and lay waste to villages. On one occasion they even stole the rajah's crown jewels and murdered his bodyguards. The ruler demanded that the culprits be found and brought to justice, yet The Thugs continued their onslaught and were never caught. The few who knew the ringleader's identity would never tell until after his death. For the leader of The Thugs, and the rajah who went to great lengths to catch him, *were one and the same person.* The ruler who demanded the capture of his nemesis during daylight hours, by night donned the attire of a robber and stole... *from himself.*[2] Just as he, we often find within ourselves a strange compulsion to become our own worst enemies.

2 *Paul Harvey's The Rest of The Story*, pp. 71-73

The most frightening aspect of a "grand illusion" is the manner in which it sets in motion a set of self-destructive behaviors. Each grand illusion, with its corresponding dominant emotion and phantom fear, creates two sets of contradictory behaviors, one intentional, the other unintentional and often completely inexplicable to the person engaging in them. This push-pull tendency within all of us constitutes one of life's most vexing and troubling mysteries. The Apostle Paul wrote almost two thousand years ago the following words: "I do not understand what I do. For what I want to do, I do not do, but what I hate I do.... For I have the desire to do what is good, but I cannot carry it out. For what I do is not the good I want to do; no, the evil I do not want to do—this I keep on doing."[3] The Apostle did not mean to imply that he could *never* do what he thought was right and good, but that he couldn't find within himself the power to *consistently* do so. Even Saint Paul struggled with the battle between intentional behaviors and unintentional compulsive ones. How much more likely are we to fight a similar battle?

The intentional behaviors are those which are consciously chosen as a strategy to combat one's phantom fear. As discussed in chapter two, these usually constitute a mask, or a role-play. For example, one who feels insecure and therefore fears abandonment above all other circumstances, will predictably take on the persona of an enabler. He or she will adopt a pattern of behavior intended to guarantee absolute indispensability to a certain key person or perhaps several different persons. The spouse of an alcoholic will, in order to avoid being deserted, become the one upon whom the alcoholic depends for the continuation of the addiction. The enabler will, in turn, rely upon the alcoholic as the one person who cannot afford to desert him,

---

3 Romans 7:20-21, New International Version

hence the title, "codependent." This codependent will lie to the addict's boss, keep up appearances with the neighbors, provide alibis, and nurse the drinker back to sobriety after each binge.

Similarly, a person carrying the illusion of inadequacy will most fear failure, and will consequently tend to become an over-achiever, intent on holding failure at bay with an obsessively intense work schedule. Such people often neglect their families, key relationships, even their health in order to ensure career success. Others can see in their eyes a desperate need for self-validation, and the obsessive fear that someone else might be seen as even more successful. Such fears are the soil in which these intentional compensatory behaviors, even obsessive-compulsive ones, sprout and thrive.

But the greater mystery lies in the *unintentional* behaviors of the illusion-bearer, behaviors which almost invariably tend to bring him what he fears most. As the prophet Job observed nearly four millennia ago, "For the thing which I greatly feared is come upon me, and that which I was afraid of is come unto me!"[4] The phantom fear has an overwhelming tendency to wrap itself in reality and beget itself. Like the Velveteen Rabbit or Pinocchio, its longing, even its destiny, is to become real. In this way, the almost inescapable inertia of one's dominant illusion is experienced: an illusion in motion tends to remain in motion, and if left unchecked becomes a self-fulfilling prophecy. *Voila!* The vexing illusion has now become a very painful reality.

My friend, Susan, described in chapter one, is a classic example. While her normal mode was that of a tireless

4 Job 3:25, King James Version

worker determined to please her boss (and everyone else, for that matter) by producing excellent results, there was also a troubling undercurrent of unintentional, even subconscious behaviors designed to do the exact opposite. Her determination to please led to an obsequiousness that repelled almost everyone. Her constant fawning and excessive desire to please literally strangled the life out of her relationships. When people, for this very reason, began to avoid her, she responded angrily, became sullen, and bought wholesale into her Grand Illusion: *I knew no one would ever accept me!* In truth (that is, in "Grander Reality"), almost everyone would have accepted her if she didn't seem so desperate for acceptance!

The effect of one's Grand Illusion is to install the aforementioned funhouse mirror in the psyche, resulting in a distorted view of ourselves. And the full time occupation of the subconscious mind is to prove that the image in the mirror is accurate. The curious afflictions of anorexia and bulimia provide excellent examples. A woman with a nice figure is somehow convinced that she is severely overweight, and diets herself into near starvation. To any outside observer, she is horribly thin, mere skin stretched over a human skeleton. But to the *inside* observer, her subconscious mind, she is still slightly too large, and thus unattractive. Objectively, she was far more attractive at her prior weight, but by some mysterious mental acrobatics the funhouse mirror reflects back to her retina a quite obese woman. Day after day her friends, coworkers, spouse, and parents tell her that she's too thin, but the illusion remains. Her phantom fear is that her imagined obesity might cause her to be rejected because of her supposed unattractiveness. And *the behavior which was supposed to be the cure actually makes her unattractive,* fulfilling the inertia of the illusion.

24

Conversely, a person who is genuinely obese may recognize that the bulk of his or her challenges in life grow directly from this propensity to overeat. Repeated fad diets and cycles of activity and inactivity may cause the person's weight to oscillate wildly throughout life. But inevitably, any lost weight is regained because the core problem, the "Grand Illusion," has never been eliminated. In many cases, the tendency to put on weight is caused by the illusion that one will never be genuinely loved. Consequently, when a person has no "special someone" to love, he or she may lose weight (the *intentional* behavior) to attract someone. Then, whether the search for a mate is successful or not, the weight is added back on (the *unintentional* behavior). Why? The subconscious goal is to prove that they were never lovable to begin with. Even if they find themselves in an authentic love relationship with someone who adores them, they generally respond by packing on more weight than ever. The act of gaining weight is a subconscious means of putting physical distance between them and their partner. The subconscious goal is to put on so much weight that the one who loves them will ultimately withdraw their love, fulfilling the inertia of the illusion. The overweight person sees himself or herself as unlovable, therefore the mind induces behaviors to ensure that this image is reinforced and confirmed as true.

It is the eternal law of life that one can never live permanently in a manner that surpasses the image he or she sees in the internal mirror. That image, or "Grand Illusion," creates a vortex which exerts an almost inescapable gravitational pull on the psyche. Day by day, year by year, a young man toils to escape his feelings of worthlessness. He works weekends, skips vacations, labors late into the night to build the life of his dreams. Yet there is a mysterious side to his personality that drives him to sabotage his own success.

Like the people of ancient Babel, he builds his tower to the stars. But from time to time he finds himself driven by an unseen force to peck away at its foundation, somehow fearing the very success he craves. A popular bumper sticker reads, "It's hard to soar with the eagles when you work with a bunch of turkeys." A more accurate adage might be, "It's hard to soar with the eagles when you *perceive yourself to be a turkey.*" Efforts to escape a low self image by simply outworking the competition and soaring above them will fail to overcome the inertia of one's Grand Illusion, because the conscious mind functions only during the waking hours, while the subconscious mind works around the clock. Though the endeavor of the conscious mind is to improve the quality of one's life, the full-time occupation of the subconscious mind is to prove that the image in the funhouse mirror is accurate.

There is within each person a civil war being fought between the conscious desire to excel and the subconscious desire to make external reality match one's grand illusions. The conscious self works valiantly to prove that the image in the mirror is false, while the subconscious mind toils below the surface to confirm it. Some easily discouraged souls never make a serious attempt to break free of the illusions that plague them. Quite the contrary, they use them as an excuse for failure, and as justification to demand sympathy or charity from friends, family, the government, or even strangers. Others vacillate between extremes of fighting the illusion and capitulating to it. Still others run from their illusions with a never-ending fury, scaling heights most only dream about, then come crashing back to earth with a shocking suddenness and finality. Even if the crash appears to make a person miserable, there is at least a sense of equilibrium and peace when society's view of a person matches his own view of himself.

Consider the case of O. J. Simpson. Why would a man so rarely blessed as he risk destroying it all by venting his rage on his ex-wife and an innocent bystander? The answer lies much deeper than the simple desire to exact revenge for unrequited love. The root cause was his Grand Illusion exerting a tremendous gravitation pull that dragged him down from his heights in order to create an inner balance, a world in which self-perception and that of others are one and the same.

O. J. Simpson was raised in the ghetto of San Francisco. His nutrition-deficient diet led to rickets, which weakened his bones to the point that his legs began to bow severely even while he feet turned inward. His mother, unable to afford proper medical care, made him wear his shoes on the wrong feet, and then attached the tip of each shoe to metal rod which forced them to point straight ahead. By the time he reached elementary school, his legs were permanently bowed, his calves shockingly thin, his head too large for his body. Other children teased him relentlessly with nicknames like "Water Head" and "Pencil Legs," which might actually be no worse than his real name, Orenthal. He joined a street gang known as the Gladiators, and three times his mother was forced to bail her young son out of jail. Afflicted deeply with the Grand Illusion of worthlessness, Simpson fought back. He rebelled against the illusion with an intensity rarely matched in this world. He became the first running back in NFL history to rush for 2,000 yards in a single season, a sportscaster, product endorser, actor, multi-millionaire, and resident of a posh Los Angeles neighborhood. And then in one colossal moment, on June 13, 1994, he returned to the wasteland from whence he had emerged decades earlier. Reduced again to poverty, the butt of jokes, locked in a California jail cell for over a year he no doubt felt a peculiar blend of despondency and peace.

Simpson experienced the exquisite pain and peculiar satisfaction that come only with congruency, the perfect alignment of the public reality and the private illusion. The agony of losing his fortune, home, careers, income, and the adulation of millions is understandable, but it is the strange sense of peace that baffles. There is an odd sense that all is right with the world, even if circumstances are atrocious, when outer reality matches one's own inner perception of it. There is a pervasive sense of satisfaction when an O. J. Simpson can say to himself, "I was right. I am just a worthless little boy from the ghetto after all." Having consciously struggled to escape the ghetto, his subconscious mind eventually won out (as it almost always does), by returning him to a self-imposed ghetto-like existence. Such is the inertia of an illusion, inherent in all six of life's Grand Illusions.

Chapter 4

The Grand Illusion of Victimization

We have become *A Nation of Victims*. Such is the conclusion of Charles J. Sykes in his book of the same title.[5] With wit and satire he provides a litany of both hilarious and tragic examples which prove his point. I have added a few of my own. Washington D.C. Mayor Marion Barry is videotaped smoking crack cocaine with a prostitute, and immediately claims that he is a victim of racism. Leonard Tose, former owner of the Philadelphia Eagles NFL franchise, walks into an Atlantic City casino and loses fourteen million dollars in a single night. Rather than express embarrassment at his foolishness, he instead files suit against the casino for allowing him to drink while gambling. A woman spills coffee in her lap and files suit against McDonald's for failing to warn her that the coffee was hot. A teenager steals a car from a private parking lot in Framingham, Massachusetts and is later killed when he wrecks the stolen vehicle. His parents then file suit against the parking lot owner for failing to prevent the theft. Clarence Thomas and Anita Hill are

5 Charles J. Sykes, *A Nation of Victims*, St. Martin's Press, 1992

29

embroiled in a public hearing with the nation watching. She claims to be a victim of sexual harassment, while he argues that he is the victim of a "high-tech lynching of a black man." Lorena Bobbitt mutilates her husband's genitalia and is exonerated because she was a victim of emotional abuse. A Philadelphia schoolteacher is fired after showing up late for work *every single day*. His lawyer files suit against the school district, claiming that the teacher was discriminated against as a handicap victim. His handicap? His lawyer argued that he suffered from "Chronic Lateness Syndrome." And so it goes....

With the comparatively recent advent of the field of neuroscience has come an unexpected and deadly consequence. Scientists studying human behavior have actually reinforced the victim mentality of our society by promulgating the view that virtually all behavior is the result of genetics. The polar opposite of Locke's *tabula rasa* philosophy, it postulates that all human conduct is, as they like to say, "hard-wired" into the central nervous system. With them, everything is predestined to a degree that would shock even the most hard-line Calvinist theologian. To them, one's morality (or lack thereof), demeanor, ambition (or passivity), confidence (or diffidence), even one's level of happiness are all predetermined at the moment of conception, and are therefore immutable. Does it somehow escape them that by their own line of reasoning they were predestined to reach this conclusion irrespective of the evidence supporting or refuting it? Consequently, even to propose the theory is a self-defeating exercise in futility.

While some who claim victim status blame their DNA, most still prefer the opposite extreme, opting for the more conventional approach and blaming environmental factors such as family, neighborhood, government and society for their lot in life. Criminals cite their impoverished childhoods, or the early loss of a parent to death, divorce, or desertion. The poor complain about lack of opportunity. Minorities point to their ethnic backgrounds as an insurmountable handicap. Meanwhile, white males have now jumped on the bandwagon complaining that they are the victims of reverse discrimination. These arguments, too, fail because many people of all races and backgrounds succeed in spite of such supposed impediments. Still other people fail, though blessed with every advantage.

The fact that millions of people cite both environment *and* heredity (whichever seems more applicable and, therefore, plausible) as proof of their helplessness belies the actual truth. The goal of this line of reasoning is to find an excuse—and therefore a justification—for one's own lack of success or happiness. In either case—environment or heredity—the outcome is the same: *no one is responsible for anything*. Fatalism becomes the ruling philosophy of the day, and success and failure are viewed as the result of pure, dumb luck. Consequently, the successful are deemed "arrogant" and "insensitive" unless they attribute their good fortune to nothing more than the outcome of a random set of fortuitous circumstances.

Whether due to genetic programming or environmental factors, millions of people view, and therefore live, their lives as though they were like locomotives, inextricably bound to a set of railroad tracks leading to a predetermined end. Feeling like feathers blown helplessly about by the fickle winds of circumstance, they assume that God, fate, or happenstance has predestined them to a life of mediocrity or worse, and there is therefore nothing that can be consciously done to change the outcome. One must hope against hope for a "big break," the appearance of Ed

McMahon on the front stoop with an oversized check, the propitious arrangement of numbers on a sequence of ping-pong balls, or a random match on the spinning dials of a slot machine. If bad luck has sentenced them to a life of misery and shame, they reason, then a spell of good luck is the only antidote.

The grand illusion of victimization is inevitably the father of despair and hopelessness. Few factors could be as de-motivating, even paralyzing, as the sense that one is powerless to improve his or her state in life. Individuals feel that they are the helpless pawns of a boss, a spouse, an unruly child, government, genetic programming, the economy, oppression, and a thousand other factors. Their view that life is fully scripted in advance becomes an excuse for failing to excel. While the feeling of helplessness breeds hopelessness, the awareness of just how much of life is genuinely under our own control is liberating and motivational. At least two of the most important influencers of life are completely under each person's control.

Attitude

When I was a small boy, there was a dead-end street in my neighborhood. It was about forty yards long, and ended at a small stream that the developer was planning to bridge so that he could build more homes on the far side. But in the interim, he used that dead-end to store construction supplies, piles of lumber, bales of shingles, etc., which made that short stretch of road a virtual Mecca for all of the children of the neighborhood to gather there and play. Upon our arrival at this makeshift playground one day we were met with a curious pile of tar balls. The builder had dumped several piles of sticky tar balls, each ball about the size and shape of a good skipping stone. To an adult, these tar balls were almost certainly the makings of a future road. But to little boys, they were ammunition! We would cram our pockets full of tar balls, and hide behind piles of lumber to fling them at each other. One day, after just such a battle, I returned home oblivious to the fact that my pockets were still filled with tar balls, and they went through the wash. And then they went through the *dryer*. There, in my mother's warm dryer, those little tar balls melted. They not only ruined that entire load of laundry, they literally paved the inside of the dryer! I don't think I'll ever forget how my mother responded: she put me bodily in the dryer with a hammer and chisel to scrape the tar out!

It would be easy to assume that the tar balls melted due to the heat produced by the clothes dryer, but this is not the entire story. Suppose, instead of putting tar balls in a dryer and heating them to 150 degrees for one hour, we put some lumps of clay in a kiln and heated them to 2,000 degrees for twelve hours. What would happen to them? They would *harden*. Don't ever allow yourself to believe that it is the "heat" applied to you by circumstances, or the economy, or your environment that causes you to melt. Heat cannot do that. The only thing heat can do is reveal your melting point; it can merely expose the stuff of which you are made. This is wonderful news for the potential "victims" of the world, because as human beings we enjoy the high privilege and incontrovertible right to choose our own melting point, to consciously select the stuff of which we are made. We do that every day of our lives, usually many times in a given day, by exercising our inalienable right to choose our attitude.

Perhaps the most important question of life is this: "Is the glass half empty, or half full?" The way a person chooses to answer that question will determine more than almost any other factor how happy or unhappy that person becomes. Attitude is life's great equalizer. It would be horribly unfair if the determining factor in one's happiness level was his or her DNA. It would be terribly unjust if one's happiness were dictated by a genetic predilection to think like Albert Einstein, jump like Michael Jordan, or sing like Madonna. What happens if you come into this world jumping like Albert Einstein, singing like Michael Jordan, and *thinking* like Madonna? Are you thereby doomed to a miserable life? No, because you still get to answer the great question for yourself: Is the glass half full or half empty? Your answer will determine to a huge degree how happy and successful you become.

While it is true that each person gets to choose the extent to which his circumstances affect his attitude, it should also be noted that a person gets no choice whatsoever in the degree to which his attitude affects his circumstances. One's attitude is "on the job" twenty-four hours a day, seven days a week, shaping the surrounding world. In my profession, I travel several times each year to Las Vegas, Nevada to perform at one of the many hotels there. In 1999, I was scheduled to perform at a new hotel in Henderson, Nevada, about a thirty-minute drive from the McCarran International Airport in Las Vegas. I always travel with large, heavy trunks in which I transport my props, and I could tell the moment the cab driver pulled up to the curb to get me that he had a bad attitude. He took one look at my luggage and sighed with exasperation. I apologetically explained that I was an entertainer with large props, and that I would be happy to help him load them in his cab. He was clearly miffed as he waved me off and snapped, "No, I'll get 'em!" He mumbled and grumbled and moaned and groaned as he wrestled the seventy-pound footlockers into the back of his mini-van. I slid into the back seat as he took his place behind the wheel and asked, "Where to?" He craned his neck to peer at me in the rear view mirror. "The new Hyatt Regency at Lake Las Vegas Resort," I replied. The cabby immediately looked deflated and buried his face in his hands. "What's wrong?" I asked. "It's so *far!*" he snapped, pointing out that it was a half-hour's drive to Henderson. I was completely taken aback by his response. I had frustrated taxi drivers in the past by requesting trips they deemed way too *short* to be worth their while, but never for a trip that was too far. I said, "Isn't that what a cab driver wants, a good fare?" "Normally, yes," he retorted, "but this is my last run of the day and I was hoping to get home at a decent hour." I offered to take another cab, but he angrily put the car in gear and pulled out into traffic, way too fast for my comfort. He mumbled and grumbled and moaned and groaned all the way to my destination about how his wife would have dinner on the table already, and that she would be angry when he came home late. When we arrived, I paid his fare, and gave him a truly rotten tip: *one dollar*. My point is this: I suspect that cab driver went straight home and told his wife that he has a bad attitude *because his passengers are lousy tippers!* He obviously had it completely backwards. His passengers are lousy tippers because he has a terrible attitude.

It would be very easy for any of us to say, "The reason I have a bad attitude at work is that my boss doesn't pay me what I'm worth." Perhaps that's true. More likely, your boss doesn't pay you what you think you're worth because you have a bad attitude! Or, more likely still, perhaps it's a little bit of both, the proverbial chicken and egg dilemma. One begets the other in a downward spiral not only at work, but in family and personal matters, as well. For the wise reader, today would be the day to strangle the chicken, or scramble the egg, and make a decision that from today forward life will be faced with a fabulous attitude. Few issues in life are more important than this one.

Is the glass half full or half empty? The answer is a simple one: *it's up to you.* No one in the world can answer that question for you. But it is the eternal law of life that if you choose to answer that question by saying, "My glass is half empty," *it will get emptier.* The consequence of a negative attitude is that you will attract bad circumstances and bad people to yourself, and over the course of your life you will drain your glass to the dregs of all the joy you could otherwise have known. But the converse is also true. If you choose to answer your question by saying, "My glass is half full," it will get fuller! By virtue of a fabulous attitude you will attract good things and good people to yourself and through the years you will fill your glass to overflowing with all of the joy that a life can contain.

A man and his three-year-old son were on a plane together. It was the boy's first flight, and he was excited, so excited that he was becoming disruptive to the other passengers. The father devised a strategy to keep his son occupied. He turned to the back of the in-flight magazine and tore out the foldout map of the world depicting all of the routes flown by that particular airline. As best he could, he tore it along geographical lines into several pieces, and mixed them up on the boy's tray table. "Put together the puzzle, son," he said. "It's a map of the world." The man hoped the toddler would stay occupied for a few minutes at least. He thumbed through the magazine for a few seconds, then glanced down and was stunned to see that the boy had already perfectly completed the map of the world. Thinking the boy might be a budding genius or a cartographical prodigy, he asked, "Son, how did you put that map of the world together so quickly?"

"It was easy, Daddy," the boy replied. "On the back of that page there was a picture of a man's head. *And when I got my head in the right place, the world came out just fine."*

Choices

If victimization is a "Grand Illusion," the grander reality must be this: the primary determining factors in the quality of a person's life are his or her own choices. The story of any given person's life is being written by his own hand, day by day, minute by minute, in the decisions he or she makes. Just as a door swings on its hinges, life turns on choices. The fodder for many a movie plot has been furnished by playing out the importance of a person's decisions, often made on the spur of the moment, yet with monumental implications. There was the choice to marry rather than break-up, the decision to take the job in Phoenix or go to work in the family business, the dilemma over whether to major in business or education, the option to indulge or to restrain ourselves. All of us can recall pivotal moments in our lives when such decisions, perhaps seemingly insignificant at the time, were made that shaped a large part of our lives. For better or worse, such pivotal moments shape lives and destinies; and their impact is almost always far greater than that of surrounding people, events, or circumstances.

The seeds of success or failure, happiness or misery, health or sickness are often sewn early in life in the form of decisions. The seminal choices children make to be obedient to their parents or to cave in to peer pressure often set the tone for a life of general well being or lawbreaking. Decisions to indulge in alcohol or drug abuse or sexual experimentation in the pubescent years may inflict blows to one's physical and mental health that linger throughout life.

37

Choices to discipline oneself and delay personal gratification until a later time frequently separate future successes from those who struggle financially throughout life. It is typical of those who make poor or mediocre choices to later in life cry that they are helpless victims of a spate of bad luck. It is also typical of them to accuse those who made wise decisions of greed and a lack of compassion. These charges are rarely true.

Follow the case of two mythical females through life. Betty and Bonnie come from similar households, growing up in the same neighborhood a few houses apart. Betty is studious, and takes her homework assignments seriously. Bonnie barely gets by, doing as little as she can possibly do and still pass. Both girls are pressured to drink, smoke pot, and experiment with mood-altering drugs. Betty refuses, while Bonnie surrenders. Betty attends high school classes diligently, but Bonnie frequently skips class to smoke cigarettes in the woods behind the school. Betty graduates with honors, a year after Bonnie drops out. Betty isn't a genius, but her grades are good enough to get her into a state university, where she applies herself for four years, working summers and weekends to make ends meet. Meanwhile, Bonnie is working as a waitress until she gets pregnant by her boyfriend, and they choose to marry at the tender age of 18. Six years later, Betty, now a college graduate and intern at a local software company marries as well, but is careful to delay motherhood another few years. Bonnie by now has three children, and her husband has long since deserted her. She lives with her parents and uses food stamps to buy groceries. Her wages of $17,000 per year are no match for Betty's $50,000 with perquisites, not to mention her husband's similar income. Betty lives in a nice home in suburbia with her two young children, while Bonnie languishes barely above the poverty line in a mobile home. Bonnie concludes that she is a helpless victim of circumstance, and that Betty got all the "breaks" in life. And Bonnie is *wrong*.

Bonnie is living the life of her choosing, which is not to imply that she would choose her current lifestyle if all she had to do was merely wave a magic wand to make a change. To the contrary, she is the product of decades of poor choices. Similarly, almost everyone is living the life of his or her own choosing. While this analysis will seem harsh to some, to the wise it will be liberating. It means that no one is on a set of railroad tracks leading inexorably to poverty, obesity, divorce, or unhappiness, because the only circumstance that is impossible to improve is the one exacerbated by a negative attitude and poor choices. Freedom comes with the rejection of the Grand Illusion of victimization, and the embracing of personal responsibility for one's own state in life.

It is quite easy to overlook the fact that people choose their own oppressors. None of us have the privilege of avoiding victimization. We do, however, enjoy the right to choose whether we endure the pain that results from disciplining ourselves, or the pain that invariably results from our unwillingness to do so. Some people pay the price of regular exercise and a bland diet to stay thin. Others pay the price of poor health for the privilege of eating anything they please and living a sedentary life. Some pay the price of entire nights of studying and writing term papers for the opportunity of graduating with honors. Others pay the price of flunking out of school for the opportunity to enjoy endless partying. Some endure the pressure of working eighty hours each week to climb the corporate ladder, and reap the rewards of senior management salaries and benefits. Most choose to pay the price of lower pay in exchange for the benefits of low stress and lots of free time. In this way we are all victims, but the wise choose to be their own "victimizers", while the foolish merely reap the unavoidable consequences of their own shortsighted choices.

Of course, there are some genuine victims, those who made wise choices all their lives only to encounter some unexpected and undeserved calamity. James Brady, former press secretary to President Ronald Reagan is one. On March 30, 1981, Brady just happened to be standing in the wrong place when John Hinckley opened fire on the President. One of those explosive bullets, dubbed "The Devastator" by its manufacturer, penetrated Brady's forehead at his left temple and lived up to its name. As it was designed to do, the bullet exploded on impact into several fragments that literally shredded the press secretary's brain. The injury was so severe that all three networks erroneously reported him dead. Now, more than twenty years later, Brady is still paralyzed on the left side of his body, suffers short-term memory loss, and slurs his speech. No reasonable person would deny that James Brady is an innocent victim. Nevertheless, he has steadfastly denied himself the luxury of this designation.

Brady was interviewed by Barbara Walters several years after the shooting. He described how one stray bullet had taken away his career, his ability to walk, his ability to control his emotions, his ability to speak clearly. Barbara Walters asked him, "Mr. Brady, are you bitter?" His answer is one that should be emblazoned on the frontal lobes of every person who has ever sought to excuse bitterness and lack of action by asserting victim status. He smiled with the part of his mouth that still functions, and said, "No. I learned a long time ago that you play the hand that's dealt you." *You play the hand that's dealt you.* What a beautiful answer! You don't get demoralized or angry because someone else was dealt a full house and you were stuck with a pair of threes. Instead, you play your pair of threes with all the enthusiasm, determination, and motivation you can muster, and that is the key to a happy life, and often to a successful one, as well.

In reality, all of us are victims of circumstances beyond our control. We all bear scars from childhood. We all enjoyed the benefits and endured the difficulties of our upbringing. We are all subject to the whims of the economy, the acts of evil people, and the decisions of government. But that which is a reality for all grows into a debilitating illusion for some. It undergoes this unfortunate transformation when we allow ourselves to believe that because we cannot control everything, we cannot control enough to make a genuine difference in the outcome, that because we cannot alter the past that we cannot seize control of our future, that because we are victims, we are therefore helpless. The moment we surrender to these false conclusions, we have thereby internalized a "Grand Illusion."

In truth, all of us hold in equal measure in the palms of our hands the single greatest purely human power in the universe. It is the ability to face any circumstance of life, no matter how onerous, with a fabulous attitude and an appropriate response. It is the willingness to accept responsibility for our own position in life, and take upon ourselves the responsibility to improve it. Even when one like James Brady is a *genuine* victim, life can shaped for the better by refusing to behave like one. If he can endure the *reality* of victimization, certainly we can thrive by rejecting the *illusion* of it. The next three chapters describe subsets of this powerful illusion of victimization.

THE GRAND ILLUSION

I am a helpless victim of circumstance.

THE GRANDER REALITY

I fully control the two most important ingredients of a successful and happy life: my attitude and my choices.

Chapter 5

The Grand Illusion
of the Windfall

The common cry of millions of Americans in recent years has been, "Give me a break!" The belief that a sudden windfall will turn their lives around has gripped the psyche of a host of people, burying them under one of life's most paralyzing illusions. A recent study showed that the three most common strategies for becoming wealthy in America are:

1) Win the lottery.
2) Become injured and sue someone.
3) Inherit money from a deceased relative.

The illusion that a sudden "big break" resulting in an influx of cash from an unexpected source will be the secret of a happy and/or successful life is ubiquitous. In reality, only a tiny fraction of America's wealthy and powerful attained their status via a windfall from lottery, lawsuit, sweepstakes, or inheritance. The vast majority got there by a very different strategy: the *slight edge*.

The illusion that sudden wealth is the answer to most of life's problems is not only false, but absurd. In fact, it is not even the best solution to money troubles. People who are poor became that way by handling money foolishly, or by living with someone who does. In other words, they *think* like poor people, and therefore slowly, inexorably sink into a morass of financial struggles or even destitution. A lifetime of choices to spend their money on lottery tickets (the state of Illinois reported in September of 2002 that the average citizen of that state spends $500 per year on lottery tickets!), or alcohol, or drugs, or questionable investments ensures that they will never have money to spare. By ending their education too soon, failing to discipline themselves, and engaging in impulse purchasing they have established a financial glass ceiling over their own heads. By failing to understand that profits are much to be preferred to wages they have ensconced themselves in a no-higher-than-middle-class existence. They purchase items they can't afford (often at exorbitant interest rates) in order to impress others. They then make the minimum payment each month on their credit cards. Poor people are poor because they (or someone close to them, such as a spouse or parent) do the things that poor people do.

Those who are wealthy, conversely, think like wealthy people, and therefore engage in behaviors that eventually produce wealth. They save their money and invest it, counting on interest for a portion of their income growth. They outwork their competition, often starting their own businesses so that they have no limit to their income. They pay off their credit card bills in full each month. They spend wisely, and seek to use their money on purchases that will generate income, or at least appreciate in value. They live well within their means so that they will always have money to spare. Most wealthy people are wealthy because they have spent a lifetime doing the things wealthy people do. These behaviors emanate from a bedrock of accurate beliefs, just as the choices of the poor originate in their illusions.

The presence or absence of monetary riches is simply evidence of a proper or improper way of thinking that existed long before. This explains why wealthy people who suddenly lose their money to a lawsuit, or the collapse of their country's economy, or fraud are usually soon wealthy again. Similarly, when a relatively poor person suddenly becomes wealthy, the money seldom lasts. In both cases, the habits acquired over a lifetime slowly take over, and cause the newly poor to grow wealthy again, and the recently rich to return to their poverty.

Compounding the problem for the *nouveau riche* is the internal mirror that portrays him or her as a poor person masquerading as a rich one. The appearance of stability and self-assurance provided by wealth is merely a facade concealing deeply seated feelings of insecurity, guilt and unworthiness. The inertia of their illusion motivates self-destructive behaviors intended to return them to the quagmire of debt and poverty they subconsciously view as their "rightful place" in society.

Far from solving all problems, sudden wealth generally creates a predicament of mammoth proportions, producing internal stress, fomenting familial conflict, and attracting an onslaught of gold-diggers. A person who prior to the windfall made thirty-five thousand dollars per year, but owed $150,000 on a home, car, and credit cards typically learns the hard way that great riches only multiply their problems. They soon discover that possessing one million dollars merely enables one to incur debts of multiple millions. What they believed was their key to happiness often opens the door to despair.

Abundant research confirms that sudden wealth does not affect long-term happiness. The landmark study cited in widespread articles was provided by Brickman, Coates, and Bulman in 1978. They compared the happiness level of 22 lottery winners with 29 paraplegics. They concluded that lottery winners were not significantly happier than the general population, and only slightly happier than those who had permanently lost the use of their legs in an accident. Researchers at Northwestern University found that although lottery winners generally described their windfall as one of the best things that had ever happened to them, their happiness did not increase. Furthermore, their everyday enjoyment of the more mundane pleasures of life such as watching television, reading books, and eating breakfast had actually *decreased,* presumably by comparison to the elation they experienced after their win. Psychologist Richard Ryan of the University of Rochester, a noted researcher in the field of human happiness, said, "If you argue that money is all you need for happiness, then those who have won lotteries should show that. But the results are a pretty mixed bag. Some of those people have wrecked their lives."[6] Indeed, fully one third of state lottery winners of jackpots of at least one million dollars eventually file for bankruptcy.[7] Generally, people return to their former level of happiness within three months of a huge windfall or serious loss.

The tendency for sudden riches to actually ruin a person's life was dubbed "Sudden Wealth Syndrome" in the

6 *Rochester Review*, "Money? Thanks, but No Thanks" Spring-Summer, 2000, Vol. 62, No. 3
7 Paul Tharp, "Lottery Raises Issues of Cents and Sensibilities," *New York Post*, 14 November, 1997

1990's "dotcom" boom, when Silicon Valley was churning out 64 millionaires each day. Some clever members of the medical community prefer the term "affluenza." An article in a British newspaper, the *Sunday Mercury*, chronicled the demise of many of that country's lottery winners. A former carpenter won 1.8 million British pounds in 1999, moved into a mansion, became a recluse, and drank himself to death. A friend commented on his final days: "For the last six weeks of his life, he existed on whiskey." A 39 year-old father of three won 2.1 million pounds, and died of a heart attack, apparently from the stress of his win, less than two years later. Another man, Roy Wilson, won 1.1 million pounds and was immediately embroiled in a family dispute about how the winnings would be distributed in the event of his death (he was 57). The family feared that Wilson's partner, Denise Hanson, 52, would get all the money. The stress associated with his win apparently contributed to his untimely death, and a legal nightmare ensued. One of his four children squandered his share of the inheritance in five months on drugs, then was jailed for breaking into his sister's home in search of more money with which to purchase heroin. His sister, Donna, said, "I hate what the lottery has done to this family. People think it brings happiness, but it has ruined our lives."

Sudden wealth is rarely a cure. Far better is the slow, relentless accumulation of wealth achieved by wise choices and personal discipline over a period of many years. When accomplished this way, the stress and confusion of "Sudden Wealth Syndrome" is averted and sufficient time for gradual discovery is allowed. Unexpected riches often serve only to magnify the foibles of their recipient, who was previously restrained in his or her excess by the lack of money. An abrupt increase in wealth simply removes all obstacles to dissipation. The recreational drug user can now afford out-

47

right addiction. The casual drinker can now fully stock a private bar in his own home. The over-spender can now bankrupt herself with risky investments and outrageous purchases.

Albert Einstein once said, "The greatest mystery on earth is compounded interest." Indeed a small investment made early in life grows at a geometric rate, imperceptibly at first, then a little more, then by leaps and bounds. Money invested at only a 10% annual return doubles in just over seven years. It doubles the original amount again in only four years, and again in two-and-a-half years. What is true of money is also true of actions.

Wise people recognize that they do not have to work twice as hard as others to excel. On the contrary, they need *only work three or four percent harder and longer* over a period of years to eventually obtain a huge advantage. An automobile traveling 61 miles per hour for eight hours will only travel eight miles further than one traveling 60 mph. But if this tiny difference is maintained over the course of a month, the gap is widened to 240 miles. In a year, the minimally faster car has opened a nearly 3,000 mile lead, and in ten years has traveled in excess of the entire circumference of the globe farther than one traveling only a tiny bit slower.

Jay Leno, host of NBC's tonight show, seemed to be in deep trouble when David Letterman made the jump to CBS to compete directly with him. Letterman was clearly winning the ratings war, but slowly Leno crept into contention, overtook him, and has won soundly for the past several years. His secret? Leno attributes his victory to his dogged perseverance, his determination to simply outwork the competition every single day. By spending his entire adult life working when his opponents were vacationing, resting, or recreating, he slowly but steadily beat them out. As Eddie Cantor said, "It takes twenty years to make an overnight success." Rather than passively waiting for a "big break" to rescue him, he simply outworked the competition by a small margin over a period of years.

For many, the key to great success will be a simple decision to work two hours longer each week, to make one additional sales call each day, to watch one less television program each evening, to rise thirty minutes earlier each morning, or exercise one more time per week. One additional date with your spouse each month can turn a marriage around. An extra twenty minutes daily with your child can cement your relationship for life. Three less soft drinks consumed each week can slim the waistline and lengthen life. The Apostle Paul, in the book of Galatians, wrote the following words: "Let us not grow weary in well-doing, for in due season we will reap, if we do not give up." He was singing the praises of the plodder, one who merely puts one foot ahead of the other day after day after day, knowing that progress is being made even if it is so tiny as to be unseen by others.

THE GRAND ILLUSION
I must rely on a "big break" to fulfill my dreams.

THE GRANDER REALITY
All I need to succeed is to maintain a slight edge over others for a long period of time.

Chapter 6

The Grand Illusion of Entitlement

Grandpa Simpson, father to Homer in the television cartoon series, *The Simpsons,* once passed a street panhandler and griped, "Everybody wants something for nothing." He then walked into his local Social Security office and shouted, "I'm old! Gimme, gimme, gimme!" While one can certainly make a strong case that the elderly are deserving of social security because most of them paid into the system throughout their working lives, it is difficult to miss the irony in the cartoon. Long gone are the days sung about by Archie and Edith Bunker, "Everybody pulled his weight. Those were the days."

Among life's most rampant and harmful illusions is the sense that one is entitled to anything other than those precious three inalienable rights described in the Declaration of Independence: life, liberty, and the pursuit of happiness. Benjamin Franklin, one of the fathers of our great country, was once heckled by a disgruntled audience member as he was giving a speech. The angry man asked, "Mr. Franklin, would you please tell me where all this happiness is that the constitution guarantees?" Franklin replied, "The constitution only guarantees the right to pursue happiness, but it is up to each individual to try to catch it for himself." And yet over the course of two centuries that foundation stone of American civilization has been turned on its head. The illusion of entitlement has wormed its way into the fabric of American society, and no wonder.

All of us are daily barraged, if not bludgeoned, with advertisements claiming: "Live at Shady Oaks. You deserve it," "You've earned a piece of the good life," or "Give yourself the trip you deserve." Does anyone ever stop to ask, "How do *they* know who deserves that fabulous vacation?" Couldn't a case be made that many of those watching these commercials or reading these ads, in fact, *don't* deserve the best, because they have simply have not earned them? How could it be that *everyone* deserves the best? Who would be left to live in the neighborhoods that were merely average, or drive the cars that cost less than $30,000? As nonsensical as the message is, it has been programmed into the American psyche and has grown deep roots there.

Businesses struggle with the pervasive attitude that employees are entitled to a job regardless of performance. Workers have come to believe that they are entitled to annual pay raises, competitive salaries, and holiday bonuses irrespective of what they produce. They expect a benefits package complete with health insurance, IRA contributions, and generous vacation allowances. They genuinely believe that promotions should be assigned on the basis of seniority rather than competence. They argue that everyone is entitled to a livable wage, while never mentioning that the converse must also be true: everyone should be responsible to earn that livable wage.

Society as a whole suffers under the weight of entitlement thinking. Citizens have become convinced that they are entitled to health care, prescription drugs, child care, food stamps, welfare payments, unemployment compensation, education, legal services, and a host of other government handouts *simply because they are alive*. They seem quite content that only the wealthy are heavily taxed while they, themselves, enjoy the benefits of the same roads, armed forces, and government agencies almost free of charge. Illegal aliens enter the country and then protest that they should be provided with all of the same government handouts given to citizens. When anyone dares mention that they have done nothing to earn those handouts, many angrily respond that they are *entitled* to them. More sobering still is the fact that the list of entitlements keeps growing. Now, many are demanding that the government provide (or at least mandate that insurance companies must provide) Viagra and contraceptives. Long gone is the expectation of an honest day's work for an honest day's pay. René Descartes made famous the statement, *"Cogito ergo sum,"* "I think, therefore I am." The modern equivalent has become, "I am, therefore I deserve."

I once spoke before a group of government employees, all of whom were managers. I stated that great leadership at times involves the ability and willingness to fire people who were clearly unproductive or uncooperative. After my presentation, a woman approached and reminded me, "This is a government operation. We can't fire people unless it's after thirty years of solid documentation." I suspect (though I am not certain) that she was exaggerating the length of time, but the fundamental illusion remains the same: the employer exists to provide job security for the employee. More accurately, their belief is that the government's primary duty is to ensure the financial security of its citizens.

This penchant for handouts from and dependency on the government, an employer or an insurer for one's security is one of the most paralyzing belief systems one can embrace. Far from providing a "helping hand," as such programs are intended to do, they instead create emotional cripples who slowly begin to believe that they have no obligation or responsibility to make their own way in life. On the contrary, they believe it is the obligation and responsibility of others to provide these things for them, and they become less and less inclined to provide for themselves.

An interesting parallel is the scion of a rich individual who has been provided for from birth. With never the need to lift a hand to provide for himself the heir develops a strong inclination toward a playboy lifestyle. While the parents *intended* to provide their child with the best of everything, they failed to account for the destructive effects of an easy life. The youngster often grows into an adult with few useful skills, little character, and no work ethic at all. Instead of providing a huge head start for their child, they have by their gifts inflicted upon him a life devoid of ambition and initiative. Far wiser was the adult who ensured that his child, however privileged, was required to earn an allowance and didn't have the world handed to him "on a silver platter," for that child will be spared the fate of those suffering under the illusion of entitlement.

Communism, the most ambitious social re-engineering experiment of the twentieth century, failed in large measure because of the effects of the grand illusion of entitlement. I traveled to Moscow not long after the fall of the Berlin wall, and while there I strolled into a Soviet grocery store. After living my entire life in the United States, it was shocking! This "full service" grocery store was about the size of an American convenience store. In the produce section, there were perhaps a dozen tomatoes, three or four heads of lettuce, eight or ten bags of carrots, and a few cucumbers. The fruit display consisted of a few apples and some brown bananas. The meat department was even sparser. Even among the dry goods, where there were many boxes of various foods, there was only a single brand of each. Seven decades of government control had created an entitlement mentality unsurpassed the world over. And the more deeply the illusion took hold in the minds and hearts of Soviet citizens, the lower their productivity became.

The attempts to now create a system of merit and free enterprise in the former Soviet republics are facing steep hurdles, because four generations of communists were steeped in the grand illusion of entitlement. They genuinely believe that it is the government's role to provide for the basic needs of the citizens, and rarely stop to consider who is supposed to provide the resources the government needs to supply them. For this reason, any communist country is doomed to financial collapse from its inception. The entitlement mentality causes people to become complacent and produce less, resulting in less revenue for the government, who must then continually feed, clothe, employ, and care for a growing population with progressively fewer resources. The entire system then slowly spirals into poverty, and eventual bankruptcy. The dilemma of the transitioning communist regimes will not be solved without a good dose of disillusionment.

THE GRAND ILLUSION
Others should provide all of my basic necessities of life.

THE GRANDER REALITY
I am entitled only to what I earn.

Chapter 7

The Grand Illusion of Misery

You are not only living the life of your choosing, as discussed in Chapter 4, you are also living a life that is indescribably wonderful. By virtue of living in the United States of America, it is safe to assume that nearly all of us are living a life that far surpasses that of the vast majority of people in the world. The fact that you are at this moment reading, demonstrates a freedom and ability not enjoyed by most of the world until recently. Indeed, the lifestyle enjoyed by those reading this book is likely far better than that experienced by the wealthiest people on earth just a century ago.

Take, for example, Versailles, the ostentatious palace of King Louis the Fourteenth of France. He was among the richest men in the world, and built a house that would show forth his grandeur for centuries to come. Consider that he possessed a home of nearly one million square feet, thousands of priceless pieces of art, a "Grand Canal" in his back yard a mile long, dotted with incredibly ornate fountains. These fountains were run by a machine (still considered one of the wonders of the world), situated several miles away on the Seine River, which pumped water through a hundred miles of pipeline to erupt high into the air for the king's enjoyment. The ceiling of each room in the palace is painted as though it were the Sistine Chapel. The grand hall is lined with huge glass mirrors, a rarity in the 18th century, imported from China. Louis managed to grow Orange trees at a latitude equal to that of southern Canada, by having his servants take them outdoors on warm days, and then return them to his "orangery" every night and each cold day. Scores of acres of beautifully manicured gardens are decorated with hundreds of exquisite sculptures. At one time 36,000 men were working to build Versailles; even with this amazing assemblage of manpower, the palace was under construction for half a century.

Now, consider what Louis did *not* possess. He possessed no toilets—not one. When "nature called," he used a pot in the corner of his room. He owned no bathtub or shower; he simply put on more perfume and powder each day to cover the stench. He enjoyed no central heat or air conditioning, no electric lights, no telephones. He traveled by horse-drawn carriage, communicated by personal messengers or mail that often took weeks to deliver. There were no weekend trips to the beach, no Wal-Marts down the street, no movie theaters. There were no automobiles, no airplanes, no railroads, nor even many paved roads. Despite his fabulous wealth, he had few of the niceties even the poor take for granted today.

The explorers Lewis and Clark provide an excellent example of how wonderful modern life actually is. They expended more than two years in traveling from St. Louis, Missouri to what is now Portland, Oregon and back. One of their team members died along the way. They traveled by canoe up the Missouri River against the current. They faced grave danger from disease, starvation, exposure, and hostiles. They crossed the snowy peaks of the Rocky Mountains of Montana on foot. And then they traced the same route back. Today, it is a simple matter to travel from St. Louis to Portland and back in a *single day,* in total comfort and safety.

Even our own grandparents grew up with no television (let alone VCRs, DVDs, and satellite dishes!), no interstate highways, no shopping malls, no computers, no microwave ovens, no fax machines, no copy machines, no portable phones, no e-mail, no Internet, no theme parks. Most of them didn't even have a private phone line, having to share one with neighbors. There were few home mortgages, and no credit cards. There were no antibiotics, no over-the-counter allergy formulas, or organ transplants. They faced a host of deadly diseases like polio, diphtheria, tetanus, typhoid fever, smallpox, whooping cough, scarlet fever, bubonic plague, and influenza that have all now been vanquished or tamed. Most of them lived and died having never traveled to Europe or Mexico, Alaska or Hawaii. A trip across the United States before the advent of air travel took six full days by train. Prior to that, the trip took *six weeks* on horseback.

The pain experienced by millions in this world is unimaginable to a resident of 21st century America. Pain to an American is a car that breaks down, a boss that is demanding, a home that is slightly smaller than the neighbors' or two kids in college at the same time. *Normal* life for much of the world is no car at all—ever, an unemployment rate near 30%, a shanty that is barely watertight, and not even knowing anyone who has gone to college. Consider the standard of living in Afghanistan or Bangladesh, the absence of basic human rights in China, the constant strife in the Balkans, or the staggering tax rates in Europe.

Many years ago on a trip to India I visited the city of Calcutta, a teeming mass of humanity in excess of ten million people, hundreds of thousands of whom are destitute. Outside my hotel a crowd of beggars lingered night and day, some with no legs, others with cleft pallets, many with no arms. Dressed in filthy rags, they repeatedly accosted those entering or leaving the Oberoi Grand Hotel with requests for money. Advised by my Indian travel guide not to be seduced by their panhandling, I refused to give them money for the first few days. But then, my heartstrings tugged by their persistence and longing gazes, I devised a test to see if the beggars were truly needy or mere grifters. After dining in the hotel one evening, I wrapped several dinner rolls in a paper napkin, walked a few feet out of the hotel, and opened it in full view. I was instantly besieged by scores of people who fought over the rolls and desperately attempted to cram one into their own mouths before others might snatch it away. Afraid of being stampeded to death, I tossed the remaining rolls in the air and ran back into the hotel where I watched in horror the mini-riot I had caused.

From the third floor room where I stayed those eight days I witnessed below me a heart-wrenching spectacle. At any given time, several people were picking through the mound of garbage produced by the hotel. Some were eating directly from the dump, others were gathering tin cans or other garbage that might be sold for a pittance. All day they came, dressed in rags, worn and haggard in appearance. But one fact riveted me: fully ten percent of those combing through the refuse were wearing a big smile and singing a happy tune all the while. They had learned the secret that is so elusive to many of us: that *life is attitude*.

Misery is quite a relative thing, which is why the misery of most people in our society is illusory. In grander reality, most people who consider themselves as miserable, unhappy, or afflicted with a less than adequate life are actually living dream lives by the standards of most. And not simply by the standards of people in centuries past, but the vast majority of people alive today. A difficult life by American standards is a wonderful existence to most others. Said another way, one man's misery is another man's paradise.

The inescapable conclusion is that misery and happiness are created not by circumstances, but by the lenses through which circumstances are viewed. Many a pauper has died blissfully happy, while many tycoons have taken their own lives, apparently overwhelmed by the reality that their great possessions brought them so little genuine happiness. Abraham Lincoln was absolutely correct when he noted that, "Most people are about as happy as they make up their minds to be."

THE GRAND ILLUSION
My life is miserable,
and I have every reason to be dissatisfied.

THE GRANDER REALITY
My life is more wonderful than 95% of the world has ever
experienced, and I have every reason to be thankful and
happy.

Chapter 8

The Grand Illusion of Self-Sufficiency

A **full pendulum swing's distance** from the grand illusion of victimization (and its related illusions of windfall, entitlement, and misery) is an opposing, but equally devastating illusion. While those laboring under the former illusion cry, "I'm a pawn in the game of life," those carrying the latter exclaim, *"You* may be a pawn, but *I'm* a king."

"I can do anything I set my mind to."

"No one can stand in my way."

"I am Superman. In fact, I'm better than Superman because no one has any Kryptonite."

"Watch my dust. I am a veritable god," they boast.

Some make such audacious claims aloud, while others merely scream them through their overbearing manner and almost offensive level of self-confidence.

They have internalized the Grand Illusion of Self-Sufficiency.

This illusion is often a perversion of the positive thinking mantra; it is an exaggeration of the mere benefits of an upbeat outlook on life to the level of invincibility. While positive thinking is definitely better than negative thinking, and will certainly boost the performance of anyone who regularly practices it, there are still limitations to its effectiveness. If a "PMA" (positive mental attitude) were as omnipotent as some over-zealous motivators seem to imply, I would be playing basketball in the NBA at this moment instead of writing a book! Those who gloss over this seemingly obvious observation are at serious risk of sowing the seeds of a mighty fall for themselves.

Those who allow themselves to believe that they are superior to others, not subject to the same flaws, failings, rules, and regulations as the "average" person frequently take risks that eventually prove to be their undoing. This is because overconfidence almost inevitably begets complacency or recklessness. When one genuinely believes that he needs no one else to succeed, and is fully autonomous and self-sufficient, he simultaneously becomes careless in his handling of what he perceives to be unnecessary details while alienating those who might otherwise rescue him from the consequences of his hubris. Such people view themselves as above the law, too smart or too powerful to be brought down by the same behaviors that ensnared "weaker" people.

Perhaps the patron saint of those so deluded would be Marie Antoinette, who voraciously consumed enough goods to support hundreds of her subjects, while condescendingly pronouncing, "Let them eat cake." Another might be Leona Helmsley, the wife of the late hotel tycoon Harry Helmsley. The so-called "Queen of Mean" treated their household servants as though they were subhuman. Consequently when she was charged with tax evasion, they were all too willing to testify against her, admitting that she was known to arrogantly quip, "Taxes are for the little people." Similar cases could be made against former presidents Richard Nixon and Bill Clinton, dictators Nikolai Ceausescu, Saddam Hussein and Slobodan Milosovich, and junk-bond traders Ivan Boesky and Michael Milken. But the reader would be wise not to assume from this list that one must be a millionaire or a head of state to fall into this trap.

Ordinary people regularly make this same mistake. They convince themselves that activities that broke up other marriages will never touch theirs. They are self-deluded with notions that *other* people might be fired for perpetual tardiness or sloppy work, but that they, themselves, are indispensable to the organization. They start believing that they should be paid for what they know rather than what they do, despite the fact that it was their actions that brought them success in the first place. They rationalize their under-reported income, their habitual smoking, their extended absences from family, their sedentary lifestyle, their penchant for procrastination. They cease doing the small things that made them successful initially, falsely reasoning that it was their own brilliance or the blessed smile of fate that pre-destined them to build a great career, a solid home, or a healthy body. Like the napping hare who lost the race to the steady tortoise, their cockiness leads to carelessness. And their self-assurance becomes their downfall.

John F. Kennedy, Jr. was raised with an understandable sense that he could accomplish anything. After all, he was a Kennedy. One can forgive him for believing that he was invincible, destined to wear the mantle of greatness that fell on his father, uncles and grandfather. It is perhaps no wonder, then, that he believed that even as a neophyte pilot he could navigate through weather that would be intimidating even to instrument rated professionals. His inappropriate confidence cost him his life, and that of his wife and her sister.

The late Jim Valvano, once the flamboyant basketball coach of North Carolina State University who led the Wolfpack to the 1983 national championship, reflected on his own tendency toward this illusion shortly before succumbing to cancer in 1993. His enthusiasm and charisma, coupled with a tireless work ethic, had been the foundation stones on which he built a remarkable career, which perhaps understandably led to the feeling that his was a charmed life, fated by the gods to become and remain outstanding. "Athletes and coaches are taught that they're special," he reminisced shortly before his death.[8] But his confidence in his own abilities had caused him to bite off more than even he could chew, and pay less attention to his basketball team. Allegations that players were violating NCAA policies, that drug use was a problem on his squad, and that he wasn't running a "tight ship" eventually eroded his superiors' support. He lost his job, became a successful analyst for ABC Sports and ESPN, and then began the battle with cancer that eventually claimed his life.

In a *Time* article published only weeks before his death, Valvano recounted the various careers that he had layered upon one another. In addition to his head coaching duties at N.C. State, he also took on the role of Athletic Director, newspaper columnist, author, radio show host, speaker, clothing designer, and others. "But it went on and on," he mused, "that insatiable desire to conquer the world.

8 Smith, Gary, *Sports Illustrated,* January 11, 1993, vol. 78, pp. 10 - 27.

I was an arrogant son of a bitch. But it wasn't just arrogance... I wanted to dare... I look back now and I see the truth in the Icarus myth. You know the story about the boy who's so proud of his wings that he flies too close to the sun, and it melts the wax, and he falls and dies? *What enables us to achieve our greatness contains the seeds of our destruction.*" (Italics mine.)

Indeed, it was his headlong lust for simultaneously living every life possible and his personal belief that he was virtually invincible and unstoppable that drove a wedge between him and those who wielded power at the university. It is a proverb that great success breeds great complacency. But beyond the illusion lies the unavoidable reality that the scant attention to detail allowed by such a breakneck pace and uncontrolled hubris will invariably become one's downfall.

Those embracing this deadly illusion often discover the hard way that unexpected circumstances have an abrupt way of bringing them back to reality. For Jim Valvano it was metastatic adenocarcinoma. For others it is left to the divorce papers, the pink slip, the insurmountable debt, or the call from the police station in the middle of the night to deliver the unmistakable message that no one is immune, no position secure, no person invincible. In times such as these, it behooves one to possess a worldview recognizing that not only do we all fall short of divine status, but we struggle even to master our humanity.

Emotional and mental health exist as a precarious balance between shame and pride. They are predicated on one's ability to exude confidence without hubris, and assertiveness without arrogance. Yet, they also require humility without abasement, and concern for others without obsequiousness. Personal inner well-being necessitates a rejection of the grand illusions of victimization (with its three related illusions) and self-sufficiency, and a commitment to explore the Grander Reality that dwells between them.

THE GRAND ILLUSION

I am special, so I can cut corners and break rules ordinary people can't afford to break.

THE GRANDER REALITY

No status is totally secure, and arrogance and complacency almost guarantee catastrophe.

Chapter 9

The Grandest Illusion: Inadequacy

I **once asked a prominent psychiatrist** what he believed were life's most debilitating illusions. "I'll tell you what the greatest one is," he answered immediately. "It's worthlessness." He continued, "Day after day people sit on my couch and tell me that deep down they feel their lives to be utterly without meaning, value and purpose." He also related to me that in his opinion, fully seventy-five percent of people, when they dare to become brutally honest, feel themselves to be below average human beings. The very concept, if it weren't so tragic, would be hilarious! How can seventy-five percent of *anything* be below average?!? Mathematically speaking, only forty-nine percent of us could be below average. And in practical terms, the vast majority of us lie near the center of the bell curve with very few degrees of separation between us. Yet, despite the fact that almost anyone can understand and accept this simple fact, merely agreeing that it is true has little impact on our self-perception. This is because the sense of inadequacy most of us feel lies much more deeply ingrained in our minds than any mere fact could be.

Instilled in us by childhood experiences, these faulty self-perceptions form a blurry mirror in which we inaccurately view ourselves. Though we may be attractive, the mirror tells us we are ugly. Though IQ examinations place us in the above average category, the mirror image shines more brightly than test scores, convincing us that we are a little more than an ambitious dim bulb. Though others may find us fascinating, the mirror convinces us that we are dull, boring, and unwanted. The first few pangs of pain experienced in childhood resulting from this illusion usually result in a retreat to a secondary illusion designed to lessen that pain.

Those secondary illusions are none other than the ones discussed so far in this book: Victimization, Windfall, Entitlement, Misery, and Self-Sufficiency. The standard coping technique engaged in by our subconscious mind is to reason in two entirely different directions. First, I pretend that my presumed inadequacy is not my fault, making me a victim. This illusion of victimization manifests itself in a host of ways, some of which were described in Chapters 4 through 7. My self-assigned victim status leads like night into day to the conclusion that my only real hopes of success lie in the boon of a windfall, or the beneficence or credulity of those I deem more fortunate than myself, and that deem me to be less fortunate than themselves. By screaming that I am entitled to "my fair share" of wealth, housing, vacation time, medical care, etc., completely irrespective of my own actions, I apply salve to my aching self-esteem. And because anyone can play the role of victim, regardless of income or status, the net result will invariably be perceived misery. The one who allows himself to indulge in victimization will constantly compare his lot in life (unfavorably) with others who seem to have more money, a bigger home, a better looking spouse, nicer kids, more kids, fewer kids, a more enjoyable lifestyle, greater freedom, better health, fewer problems, etc. And the predictable outcome will be sadness, bitterness, and *misery*. The grand illusion of victimization, with its consequent secondary illusions, produces *nothing:* no motivation, no drive, no upward mobility, no promotions, no raises, no nice cars, no dream homes. Its adherents doom themselves to wallow helplessly in the mire of mediocrity in scant hopes of rescue by a grinning Ed McMahon, a good poker hand, or a guilt-ridden social worker.

A second more noble, but no more helpful, secondary illusion emerges from the depths of low self-esteem: self-sufficiency. Rather than fully capitulating to a lifestyle of passivity and blame, the psyche on occasion musters the fortitude to repress feelings of worthlessness with an outright lie. Like a Phoenix rising from the ashes, the defiant conscious mind beats back the voices of hopelessness and declares, "I am a god!" In this act of heroic denial, the seeds for a mighty fall are sewn.

Those who struggle inwardly with feelings of worthlessness, yet opt to repress rather than eradicate them, set themselves up for a crash of epic proportions. By all outward appearances, such a person is the quintessential overachiever, driven to excel by unseen forces. Obsessed with proving the inner voices of inadequacy wrong, this particular illusionist toils relentlessly, resisting sleep, abjuring vacations, sacrificing relationships and health in the inexorable pursuit of a degree of success that will silence the demons once and for all. But in spite of all their efforts, the voices return, the doubts resurface, the insecurity remains. Despite sometimes amazing results, the sense that one is not an actual success, but a fortunate imposter lingers. Fears that the trappings of success might prove to be a mere house of cards and come tumbling down haunt this person. And the fears are usually justified, because they become a self-fulfilling prophecy.

The analysis of O.J. Simpson's mammoth collapse in Chapter 3 is only one in a seemingly endless litany of superstars who achieved their success by running *away* from their fears of inadequacy, rather than *towards* their innate sense of greatness. The rise and fall of Tonya Harding, Dennis Rodman, Pete Rose, Michael Jackson, Reggie Jackson, Jimmy Swaggert, Jim Bakker, and a host of others illustrates the power of this grandest of all illusions. Like a stock whose price greatly exceeds its value, it is due for a tremendous crash, a "correction" as brokers refer to it.

Perhaps no recent (and seemingly never-ending) saga more graphically illustrates this principle than the career of boxer Mike Tyson. His boxing prowess at one time earned him over thirty million dollars for a single fight, yet he apparently never saw himself as much more than a minimum wage manual laborer. Consequently, his psyche is perpetually torn between the conscious desire to succeed and to enjoy the fruits of that success, and the subconscious desire to demonstrate that his terrible self-image is correct. And so, he swings wildly from success to failure, freedom to prison, from heavyweight champion to the idiot who bit Evander Holyfield's ear nearly off, from comeback kid to the wacko who allegedly assaulted a woman in a bar and threatened a motorist on the freeway. The anxiety created by the wide disparity between his reality and his illusion predictably results in repeated attempts to sabotage his own success. And the attempts will continue until his life has been ruined in sufficient degree to match his self-image, or until he becomes *dis*-illusioned.

The key to shattering this grandest of all illusions is not to capitulate to it, nor merely to repress it. The solution is to trade in the internal funhouse mirror for one that gives an accurate reflection. A former governor of the state of Tennessee named Ben Hooper tells an oft-told but moving story. Hooper grew up in the hills of Tennessee as the illegitimate son of a poor country woman. In those days, illegitimacy carried with it a serious stigma, and the children at school referred to him simply as "the bastard." As he walked about town he could feel the disapproving stares of the townsfolk, who made a sport of guessing who the boy's father might be. Ben Hooper had no idea who his father was, but he knew who he, himself was: poor white trash.

There is little doubt that this grand illusion of worthlessness would have played itself out in a life to match were it not for one event that took place in his life when he was twelve years old. He attended a small church called Laurel Springs Christian Church, and made it his habit to arrive late and leave early to avoid contact with judgmental parishioners. One Sunday, however, he failed to leave early enough and was caught in the crowd as they filed out. He felt a "heavy hand" on his shoulder, and turned to see that it was the minister, who said loudly, "Ben Hooper, whose boy are you anyway?" Ben was humiliated. He felt the minister was making fun of him just as everyone else did. The minister asked again, "Ben Hooper, whose boy are you?" The preacher studied the boy's face as though he was about to attempt yet another mortifying guess about the identity of his father. Then slowly, the minister's expression changed. He began to smile. He said, "I know whose boy you are. The family resemblance is unmistakable. Ben Hooper, you are a son of God! Now go claim your inheritance." Decades later, with tears in his eyes, Ben Hooper would look back at that experience and declare, "That was the day I became the governor of Tennessee."[9] Ben Hooper's life changed that morning because that was the day he was disillusioned. That was the day he saw himself as he really is. Your life, too, will begin anew the day you dare to walk away from your grand illusions into an even grander reality.

THE GRAND ILLUSION

My life is fundamentally without meaning, purpose, and value.

THE GRANDER REALITY

I am a whole, capable, competent human being of inestimable value, with staggering potential to meet the challenges of life.

9 *Craddock Stories*, Michael Graves and Richard F. Ward, editors. Chalice Press, 2001.

Chapter 10

Dis-illusionment:
The First Step Toward Grand Reality

An old legend tells how hunters of old captured and killed monkeys for their prized meat in the jungles of Africa. I've been unable to document whether it is actually true, but the story is quite illustrative regardless. The hunter would supposedly drill a hole in the end of a coconut, pour out the milk, and force a few walnuts through the opening. The coconut would then be tied to a tree and left in the jungle. An unfortunate monkey who happened to be in the area would reach through the hole to retrieve the tasty treat, but while grasping the nuts his fist was too large to fit back through the opening. The monkey could easily escape by simply letting go, but instead would scream, claw, gouge, and even pull his arm out of joint, clinging tenaciously to the prized snack. The hunter would then wait for the simian to fall asleep, still clutching the walnuts, and make an easy task of clubbing his prey to death.

Low self-expectations are much like those walnuts. There is great security in holding fast to the belief that one is mediocre or worse. If one never expects to be a millionaire, an author, a CEO, or a celebrity, then failure to achieve those pinnacles is relatively painless. If one lives an entire lifetime expecting to die in obscurity, never having excelled at anything, then success may be easily redefined as merely paying the bills and growing older. In setting low goals (or no goals at all) one is insulated from the potential pain and embarrassment of falling short of them. In one's white-knuckled grip on the "walnuts" there is protection from the threat of failure, but self-doubt is thereby transformed into a self-made prison. And it is a great tragedy to dwell for a lifetime in a jail cell of one's own making, all the while possessing—but never using—the key that guarantees one's release.

Life has a way of foisting damaging "walnuts" upon us all. Here are some notable examples:

Napoleon Bonaparte had the dubious distinction of finishing forty-second out of a graduating class of forty-three in military school.

Thomas Edison as a boy was repeatedly told by his own father that he was "stupid."

The philosopher **David Hume** was described by his mother as "uncommonly weak-minded."

Albert Einstein was nicknamed the "dumkopf" by his elementary school teachers.

Louis Pasteur was described by a schoolteacher as "the meekest, mildest, least-promising student in my class."

Rod Serling wrote and marketed forty short stories before he sold even one, and *The Twilight Zone* was born.

76

Sir Walter Scott was rated a dunce as a child.

Zane Grey was fired from his first five newspaper jobs, but eventually became one of the most prolific writers in American history.

The great explorer and aviation pioneer, **Admiral Richard Byrd**, crash-landed in his first two attempts to solo an airplane.

Walt Disney was fired from his first newspaper job, being told he had "little talent as an artist."

The first pass ever thrown in an NFL game by **Johnny Unitas** was intercepted and returned for a touchdown. The next time he touched the ball he fumbled it, and it was recovered by the opposition in the end zone for a touchdown.

"Colonel" Harlan Sanders was a colossal failure throughout his life, and used his first social security check to open a restaurant he called "Kentucky Fried Chicken."

Cesar Ritz was fired from his first hotel job by a boss who told him he had "no flair for the hospitality industry."

Clint Eastwood was fired in 1959 by Universal Studios because his Adam's apple was too big.

Burt Reynolds was fired by Universal the very same day because they said he had "no talent as an actor."

Norma Jean Baker (the future **Marilyn Monroe**) was told by Emmeline Snively, Director of the Blue Book Modeling Agency, "You'd better learn secretarial work or else get married."

The Beatles were turned down by Decca Recording Company in 1962 with these words: "We don't like their sound. Guitar groups are on the way out."

Buddy Holly was called "The biggest no-talent I've ever worked with" by Paul Cohen, also of Decca Records.

Elvis Presley was fired in 1954 from "The Grand Ole Opry" after just one performance. The manager of the famed country music venue, Jimmy Denny, told him, "You ain't going nowhere, son. You should go back to truck driving."

Emmitt Smith, one of the greatest running backs in the history of professional football was recruited out of high school by the University of Florida. Recruiting guru Max Emfinger said of the high school senior, "Emmitt Smith is not big, he's not fast, and he can't get around the corner. When he falls flat on his face at Florida, remember where you heard it first."

Lucille Ball was told by her first drama teacher in 1927, "Try any other profession. Any other."

Wilma Rudolph contracted scarlet fever at the age of 4, leaving her left leg paralyzed. By age 13, she had managed to walk, and decided to become a runner. She finished dead last in every race for several years. Eventually she won three gold medals in track and field.

Phyllis Diller was a housemaid until the age of 37.

Setbacks, criticisms, and mistakes like these are likely to burden anyone with entire bags of "walnuts," and the very human tendency to cling doggedly to the convenient excuses they provide. By the time we reach adulthood, each of us is laden with bushel baskets full self-doubts. But along with maturity also comes a gift that is indescribably wonderful: *the option to let go of them.* All of the men and women listed above received their share (and in some cases, *more* than their share) of walnuts; but somewhere in the jungle of life they mustered the courage to release them, leave them behind, and profoundly believe in themselves. Freedom comes when one dares to let go and experience the exhilarating liberty of high self-expectations, the unfettered delight of dreaming big dreams and fully anticipating their realization.

To be sure, returning to Kansas from a lifetime in Oz is no simple matter; it's far more complicated than merely clicking one's heels together and reciting, "There's no place like home." But it's also not so difficult as to be a hopeless endeavor. Far from it. There are at least three steps necessary to make your trip back into the real world a certainty.

Control Your Self-talk

Few factors are so predictive of an individual's future success or failure than the words he or she continually says (silently, for the most part) to himself or herself. *"I'm so stupid!"* the mind says every time a mistake is made. The mantra is repeated daily for decades, hard-wiring a crippling chimera into the psyche. *"I'll always be fat." "No one could ever really love me." "I'm a loser." "I'll never be able to save any money."* These messages, with a thousand variations on each theme, are not merely responses to circumstances and reflections of an already weak self-concept, but are harbingers of worse things to come. Their constant repetition drowns out almost every piece of evidence to the contrary.

Success is not therefore interpreted by the mind as proof that the illusion of incompetence is incorrect, but is rather seen as an anomaly, an aberration, a fleeting error of chance that will soon be rectified. Tremendous weight loss, when viewed through the lens of one's illusion, is seen as an ephemeral reprieve, not a fundamental shift in reality. The discovery of true love is not regarded as evidence that I am lovable after all, but is seen as proof that the lover does not really know me well enough to reject me yet. Mere facts generally make little or no lasting positive change to one's self-image. A conscious strategy to silence the negative voices, however, constitutes a gigantic step forward in the process.

Change begins when an individual makes a commitment to change the mind's subliminal lies into verities. For example, the subconscious tends to speak in extreme categories which are seldom true. When a mistake is made, the old tapes in one's head begin to play the same errant message: *"I'm so stupid! I must be the stupidest person in the world."* Such a message is obviously a gross exaggeration, but knowing this simple fact does nothing to temper, let alone erase the false messages. Like an audio tape, the best way to erase the current message is to record over it. The new recording should be a more accurate message: *"I'm not a genius, but all-in-all I'm an intelligent person who is fully capable of functioning successfully in the world. I made a mistake but everyone else makes mistakes, too."* Each time the false message manifests itself, it must be instantly rebuffed with its truer counterpart.

Similar false messages, along with their usual effects and more accurate replacements are listed below.

False message: *"I'm so homely no one will ever want to*

80

date me, let alone marry me."

Effect: The result of playing the loop-tape containing this message will be a lack of confidence in the presence of potential suitors or an avoidance of them altogether, resulting in fewer dates and a reinforcement of the already firmly entrenched illusion.

True replacement: *"I'm not gorgeous, but very few people are. And lots of people who look no better than I do are happily married. There are many people who would be happy to have me for a spouse."*

False message: *"I'm the most boring person in the world. No wonder no one wants to be my friend."*

Effect: Hearing this message over and over again motivates one to become invisible, to withdraw, and to become a recluse. Parties are avoided whenever possible. When forced to attend, this illusionist is the classic wallflower. Loneliness is the most salient emotion experienced.

True replacement: *"I may not be the life of the party, but most other people aren't either. Millions of people in the world are lonely and looking for a friend just like me."*

False message: *"I'm just a no-talent loser. I can't do anything right."*

Effect: The constant repetition of this myth leads to a degree of passivity that can be devastating to a career. The refusal to become aggressively proactive in the face of difficulty often leads to the very failure one fears, and the resulting diffidence is unattractive to a potential employer or client.

True replacement: *"I may not have superstar talents, but I do have many abilities and strong points. I wish I were more talented, but I've done many good things in my life and will do a great many more in the future."*

These suggested replacement sentences serve as models upon which to base your own statements. They not only represent an improvement of the existing messages because they are true, but they also have the added advantage of being *helpful*. By making a habit of telling yourself the truth, you will slowly replace the debilitating negative voices in your head.

Fan the Flames

Successful people almost always share one quality in common: their ability to stay motivated and enthusiastic. Setbacks and obstacles may deflate them slightly and temporarily, but the net effect of any difficulty is to incite great people to even higher levels of effort and quality. For some, this resiliency is instinctive; for most, it must be fostered. In order to reverse the damaging effects of years of negative programming, specific tactics for arousing and maintaining a high level of motivation are necessary. Care must be taken not to allow discouragement to invade and dominate one's thoughts, because unmotivated time is wasted time.

A conscious strategy of exposing oneself to sources of motivational content and energy is one of the great keys to reversing the negative momentum created by one's grand illusions. The beneficial effects of a positive attitude have already been discussed in Chapter 4, and need not be expounded upon again. But in addition to guarding one's outlook, there are several steps that may be taken to fan the flames of one's enthusiasm.

1) Reading good books—Few practices are as beneficial to one's mental outlook and emotional well-being as the continual positive reinforcement provided by motivational books. One could spend a lifetime reading and re-reading the classics in the field, let alone the steady flow of new works occupying the shelves of the "self-help" section of local bookstores. Spurred on by a refreshing stream of ideas, content, moving stories, and insights, you will sense a renascent passion for excellence and success. Many highly successful people carry a book with them always, to make valuable use of time waiting in lines, sitting on planes, or dining alone. Investing time that others waste is often the difference between success and failure.

2) Attending seminars—Attending a motivational or training conference at least once each year can be an invaluable catalyst to greater productivity and renewed enthusiasm. Such seminars may be sponsored by your company, or by an association to which you belong. Others travel from city to city and are advertised widely in print and broadcast media. Frequently the boss will pick up the tab on such conferences.

3) Listening to tapes—For the busy person, audio tapes may be the best source of reinvigorating information. Recorded messages from the world's most dynamic speakers and spectacular successes can be played in your car, home, or office with little effort. They hold the added benefit of allowing you to double your time, absorbing helpful information while driving, doing laundry, or watching the kids. Such tapes can be purchased at the conferences described above, or ordered from hundreds of professional speakers and trainers across the country. A few can be purchased from book stores.

4) Spending time with motivated people—By making an effort to spend time with people who naturally inspire you or stimulate you with creative ideas, you can feed off their enthusiasm to keep your own alive. We all evidence the peculiar human tendency to rise up to or fall down to the level of our most frequent companions, which is why it is not overstating the case to say that by choosing your friends, you are also choosing your destiny. Highly successful people habitually rub shoulders with those who incite them to further success.

Challenge Your Phantom Fear

The surest way of exposing your fears as mere apparitions, figments of your imagination, is to challenge them in a forthright manner. By deliberately placing yourself squarely in the path of what you secretly fear most, you quickly unmask their illusory nature. Just as the villain in a video game poses no threat to anyone outside its contrived world of electronic circuitry and computer programming, the phantom fear exists only in the imagination and is therefore powerless against those who choose to live in another realm: reality.

The acts of correcting your self-talk and rousing your enthusiasm should give you the courage to walk directly into the teeth of what you fear most. If it is rejection you fear, you must as an act of sheer will put yourself boldly and repeatedly in circumstances that heretofore have been intimidating, or even paralyzing. If it is failure that seizes you with panic, you must courageously attempt to make serious progress in your career. Place yourself in a position where colossal failure is at least a mathematical possibility, eschewing the perceived safety of the inaction, and thereby opening the door to the prospects of wonderful success.

No football player ever scored a touchdown while sitting on the sidelines. But by placing himself in a position to catch the winning pass, a receiver voluntarily puts himself in jeopardy of dropping it. No basketball player ever sank the winning basket from the bench, but by taking the shot they put themselves in great peril of missing it. No baseball player ever hit a grand slam from the dugout, but with the opportunity for glory also comes the danger of striking out. And no person ever experienced the "thrill of victory" without mustering the courage to at least risk enduring the "agony of defeat." No one ever fulfilled his or her dreams while enjoying the relative safety of sitting on the sidelines never even attempting to get into the game. Forever hidden within the very concept of great success lurks the potential for monumental failure. The risk of the latter is intrinsic to the hope of the former.

THE GRAND ILLUSION
The key to making a lasting improvement in my life is discipline.

THE GRANDER REALITY
You change who you are and what you do by first changing what you believe; discipline is then the result of accurate beliefs.

Chapter 11

Re-illusionment:

The Path to Grander Reality

The first ten chapters of this book have detailed the processes required to break and render impotent the debilitating power of psychological illusions. However, to assume that illusions are therefore *always* damaging to emotional and mental well-being would be false. In this final chapter, we will take the all-important step of harnessing the considerable power of illusions to our benefit. The natural tendency of an illusion to gradually ooze its way out of our mouths, fingertips and feet to recreate the real world in its own image applies to positive illusions as well as negative ones. Thus, by deliberately choosing and carefully planting therapeutic or pleasant illusions in our subconscious minds we can set in motion a process with inevitably corrective results. This is accomplished by "tricking" your own mind, a process I call "re-illusionment."

The conscious mind of a healthy person places a hard wall of demarcation between that which is real and that which is imaginary. When that wall is breached, mental illness is present and therapy or psychotropic drugs are required. The subconscious mind of a normal person, however, is incapable of distinguishing between reality and imagination, a simple fact, which holds the key to erasing harmful recordings from our minds, and replacing them with motivational and inspiring messages. These germinating positive illusions will then quite naturally engage in their own relentless quest to become real, prompting a different set of behaviors destined to make these new "delusions of grandeur" slowly develop into grand realities. The act of planting and nurturing the seeds of the fresh illusions occurs through a practice of habitual and vivid imagination.

Because the psyche does not differentiate between the real and the unreal, the act of vividly imagining success in any endeavor affects self-esteem with about the same impact that actual success does. For example, winning the Heisman Trophy (given annually to the best college football player in America) would surely give a young man a measure of confidence that would have some residual effect for the remainder of his life. Similarly, being crowned "Miss America" cannot help but bolster a young woman's self-esteem somewhat, and there will almost certainly be a lasting impact from that outward affirmation of her beauty, charm, talent, and poise. But the psychological benefits of such victories decrease exponentially with time in the mind of a person with low self-esteem because the victory is momentary, while the crippling illusions and negative voices remain. However, by daily (even if only for a few moments) reliving the glory of those successes in vivid exultant memories the negative voices can slowly be drowned out and replaced. But what if one has no such victories to relive? After all, there is only one Heisman Trophy and a single Miss America crown handed out each year.

The truly fabulous news is that due to the unique

nature of the subconscious mind, one does not have to actually win the Heisman Trophy or be crowned Miss America to enjoy the same benefits of doing so. One must only be able to vividly *imagine* what such a victory would be like to force the same positive programming into the recesses of the mind. This is accomplished most effectively when one imagines a victory or achievement so vibrantly that one feels the same emotion as one who as actually lived out the dream. I have coined the term "emotionation" to describe this activity. Several examples may be cited to demonstrate the powerful effects of this principle.

In April of 1958, the First International Tchaikovsky Competition was won by the incomparable Van Cliburn. Second place was held by a little-known nineteen year-old Chinese pianist by the name of Liu Shih-kun, who subsequently returned to China in relative obscurity. But the so-called "cultural revolution" was brewing in China, outlawing the works of all western musicians including Mozart, Bach, and Beethoven. For refusing to renounce his music, Shih-kun was imprisoned, and might still be incarcerated were it not for U.S. President Richard Nixon's efforts to open communication channels to the great Asian power. For propaganda purposes, Shih-kun was briefly released and asked to play in Peking with the Philadelphia Philharmonic. His brilliant performance was astounding since he had not touched a piano in six years. His secret? For all that time in a tiny prison cell he played the piano *in his mind*. The very act of imagining playing a piano programmed his mind as though he were actually doing so.

Scores of fascinating experiments involving athletics have also affirmed the power of visualization. In one landmark study, several men (all of whom were basketball novices) were broken into three groups and asked to shoot free throws. Each group averaged about a 43% success rate. The members of group one were sent home with no instructions other than to return one week later. Group two was told to shoot ten free throws each day before returning one week later. Group three was told not to touch a basketball, but to *mentally* shoot and make ten free throws each day, and to return one week later. Group one, as expected, showed no improvement. Group two had increased their free throw percentage to nearly 60%. Group three, without ever actually practicing, had improved to 57%, only 3 percentage points less than those who actually shot practice free throws each day! The mentally simulated free throws impacted and programmed the subconscious mind almost as much as the act of shooting them had.

Olympic Gold-medalist gymnast Mary Lou Retton was taught to visualize every single movement in her programs before performing a single one. Star NFL running back Emmitt Smith has spoken openly of his habit of visualizing himself dodging tacklers and running over opposing defensive backs before each game. The habit of using mental imagery to improve performance is a well-accepted fact in the field of athletics.

In 1985, sports psychologists Woolfolk, Parrish, and Murphy conducted an experiment with novice golfers. Subjects were divided into three categories, a positive imagery group, a negative imagery group, and a control group. Those in the positive imagery group were told to imagine the ball rolling right into the cup before each putt. The negative imagery group was told to imagine the ball narrowly missing the cup, again before each putt. The control group was merely told to try to make each shot. The positive imagery group improved their success rate by 30.4%, while the negative imagery group saw their accuracy fall by 21.2%, a staggering statistical difference. Such is the power of imagination.

"Emotionation," however, is even more powerful because the results last much longer. Any event that is fraught with emotion is riveted much more permanently in the memory than an event which is devoid of emotion tends to be. For example, the memories of a funeral or wedding of someone we love deeply are much more vivid years later than the recollections of a funeral or wedding of someone we barely knew. One forever remembers hitting the winning shot in a basketball game because of the elation and celebration that accompanied it. But the thousands of shots that went in, but did not result in any emotion, have long since been forgotten.

Likewise, events that produce strong feelings are much more likely to affect behavior years after they occurred. The cager who won the championship with his last-second shot in high school will likely be much more eager to chance the winning (or losing) shot in college. Negatively, a traumatic incident such as a robbery or a rape will significantly influence a person's actions for many years hence. This is why imagination alone is insufficient to effect a long term improvement in self-esteem. *The imagery engaged in must be so intense as to produce powerful feelings.*

A lasting change in self-perception, and therefore (eventually) in behavior can be created by the discipline of "emotionation." By setting aside a minute or two each day to passionately envision succeeding in business, being the life of the party, attracting a mate, or showing off your tight waist at the beach you can reprogram your subconscious mind to make your dreams a reality.

Just as positive images can program your psyche to produce beneficial changes in behavior and performance, negative imagery can have a similar deleterious effect. For example, allowing yourself to harbor fears of open humiliation before giving a speech to your civic club, presenting a selection at a recital, or singing a solo at your church will enter the mind with the same ferocity as an actual public disgrace. Unchecked anxieties about embarrassing oneself in a job interview, at a dinner party, or on a date create a predisposition to make one's fears a mortifying reality. Care must be taken to immediately push such negative imaginings out of the mind and consciously replace them with purposeful and clear visions of success, eloquence, and charm.

Replacing one's illusions with reality is always helpful, because living with the truth is forever conducive to making wise decisions. This seminal act of disillusionment comprises the first real step to arresting self-destructive and non-productive behaviors. But it is only the first step, and one should not be content with merely ceasing a gradual downhill slide into mediocrity or ignominy. It is not enough to avoid going backward by merely learning to stand still, because Grand Reality can be turned into an even Grander Reality. By embracing new illusions and nurturing them as readily as you once unwittingly reinforced the harmful illusions that crippled you, you can begin to harness the inertia of your new illusions in a positive direction. Replacing a few of your illusions with new, carefully chosen positive illusions is life's most potent formula for lasting change.

About the Author

Billy Riggs, master illusionist and gifted public speaker, is the former pastor of one of America's fastest growing churches. He holds two master's degrees, and is the author of *The Twelve Immutable Laws of Humor*. He has been a featured entertainer on ten cruise ships, and has spoken before hundreds of audiences in North America, Africa, Asia, and Europe. His blend of comedy, magic, and motivation has been a popular keynote for companies like IBM, Hyatt Hotels, Poulan, General Mills, GTE, Georgia Pacific, DuPont, State Farm, Amway, The Hartford, and scores of others. Programs are available on sales, leadership, customer service, education, attitude, and performance enhancement.

Booking information:
(800) 299-5591
Agent@BillyRiggs.com

Tapes, books, CDs, and videos by Billy Riggs
may be purchased at:
(800) 203-0720 or
www.BillyRiggs.com/gproducts.html